LEAN OUT

LEAN OUT

How to Dismantle the Corporate Barriers that Hold Women Back

Maureen F. Fitzgerald, PhD

CENTERPOINT MEDIA

Lean Out: How to Dismantle the Corporate Barriers that Hold Women Back
Copyright © 2016 by Maureen F. Fitzgerald

All rights reserved. No part of this publication may be used, reproduced, stored or transmitted in any manner whatsoever without prior written permission from the publisher, except in the case of brief quotations embodied in reviews.

For information:
CenterPoint Media
www.CenterPointInc.com

LIBRARY AND ARCHIVES CANADA CATALOGUING IN PUBLICATION
Fitzgerald, Maureen F., author
     Lean out : how to dismantle the corporate barriers that hold women back / Maureen F. Fitzgerald.

Includes bibliographical references.
Issued in print and electronic formats.

ISBN 978-0-9939840-4-4 (paperback).
ISBN 978-1-988072-02-9 (ebook)

1. Discrimination in employment. 2. Glass ceiling (Employment discrimination). 3. Women --Employment. 4. Work-life balance. I. Title.

HD6060.F58 2016   331.4'133   C2015-905719-1
                                            C2015-905720-5

Edited by: Ann Macaulay and Catherine Leek
Layout and design: Maureen Cutajar, Go Published
Cover design: Christine Unterthiner, Pilot Brands
Cover photo: www.Phototobinphotography.com
Cover Image: Created by Lorie Shaull, the Noun Project

"All truth passes through three stages.
First it is ridiculed. Second, it is violently opposed.
Third, it is accepted as being self-evident."
~ Arthur Schopenhauer

Contents

Preface		1
Introduction		7
Part One	**We Can't See It Because It's Glass**	11
1.	Admit There Is a Glass Ceiling	13
2.	Stop Telling Women to Lean In	19
3.	Don't Fall for the Pipeline Theory	25
4.	Ask Women Why They Really Leave	29
5.	Notice the Absurd Expectations We Place on Women	35
Part Two	**There Is Nothing Wrong with You**	39
6.	Question the Tightrope of Double Binds	41
7.	Don't Expect Women to Be Mini-Men	45
8.	Question Why Women Need More Courage	49
9.	Reject Outdated Stereotypes	55
10.	Stop Asking Women to Speak Louder	61
Part Three	**Policies Do Make a Difference**	65
11.	Pay and Promote Women Fairly	67
12.	Make Flexible, Part-Time and Shared Work the Norm	73
13.	Don't Blame Women for Self-Sabotage	79
14.	Deal with Discrimination and Sexism	85
15.	Stop Sexual Harassment	93

Part Four	If We Really Want Women to Succeed	97
	16. Provide Access to Mentors, Networks and Women	99
	17. Provide Support for Life and Family	105
	18. Encourage Women to Seek Power	111
	19. Never Say Women Have Come Far Enough	119
	20. Value Feminine Strengths	125

Conclusion		**131**
Lean Out: A Manifesto for Work Equality		**135**
Appendix A	The Business Case for Advancing Women	**137**
Appendix B	The Women's Leadership Gap	**141**
Selected Bibliography		**149**
About the Author		**155**

Preface

"Enough about the glass ceiling. It's time to redesign the building so that women and men at all levels can be good employees and good family members." ~ Ellen Bravo

I have always believed in gender equality. I had parents who told me that the sky was the limit. I went to the most prestigious universities and was selected for the most amazing jobs. For the bulk of my career I refused to admit that there were any barriers that held me back.

As an accountant, a lawyer and a professor, I never felt I was being treated unfairly. I was thrilled to earn good money and felt like I was contributing. In fact, I tried to convince younger women that the glass ceiling was all in their minds. I urged women to vigorously compete head-to-head with men and "may the best man win." I would never admit that I was a feminist or that I had friends who were feminists and I frankly found it distasteful to complain or whine. But then I had my eyes opened.

My Story

Around 10 years ago, at the pinnacle of my law career, I returned to work after a short maternity leave, only to discover that there had been a "re-org." My boss told me that I had been moved into a new position and would get a minor raise. Although he called it a promotion, it was a mundane job with no growth potential. It required that I report to three (not one) male bosses, two of whom used to be at my level and, to top it off, I was now moved to an interior office with no windows. I felt as though I was being squeezed out of my high-paying job as a lawyer into a tiny box. As a result, my world completely shattered.

All the myths I had told myself for 20 years about equality and fairness came into focus and I could no longer pretend. It was as if all of a sudden I came face to face with all the lies I had lived by.

I felt as if I had been naive or blind. I had fallen hook, line and sinker for the propaganda that women are completely equal. I accepted the lie that because I was a lawyer, I had equal opportunities and unlimited choices.

I did not mind when I didn't get invited to client lunches. I did not care when all the male lawyers played golf in the middle of the day (even though I could play better than most of them). I did not really notice when my male peers got more of the interesting files. I did not mind that I worked all alone in the office until the wee hours of the morning. I was flattered when I was asked to do pro-bono projects (that men steered clear of). I silently accepted requests to take notes at meetings and serve coffee, chalking it up to rites of passage.

20/20 Hindsight

Looking back, I see things quite differently. Even as a young star, I was always on my toes, rarely relaxed and often stressed. I worked obscene hours and met ridiculous deadlines. I was kept out of influential meetings and projects. People with fewer skills than me were promoted without explanation. I was constantly working overtime to make up for the time I took off to take my children to the dentist or doctor or teacher professional days. I was overlooked for obvious promotions. I had to fight for the smallest raise. I was given menial work. And when I mentioned this observation to my peers, I usually got a shoulder shrug or a comment like, "Suck it up, buttercup" or "Welcome to the real world."

And to make matters worse, I blamed myself for all these happenings. I recall often thinking that there must be something terribly wrong with me. Maybe I really was difficult to get along with? Maybe I was not as smart as I thought? Maybe I had offended someone important? And because I thought it was my fault entirely, I dared not complain. I felt ashamed and I lowered my expectations. I lowered my self-esteem, I bent my head down and I worked even harder. I chose to remain blind and convinced myself that I just needed to be faster and tougher.

I had absolutely no idea that there were barriers holding me (and most other women) back and I had no idea how invisible, destructive and resilient they were.

The Missing Piece

Once I began research for this book I quickly realized that I was not alone. This situation was not personal to me. I was simply a cog caught in the wheel of the invisible systems and institutions that hold many women back. Even though as a lawyer I knew about sexism and discrimination, I had no idea of the depth of the problem until I felt the sting on a personal level. It was not until I felt the pain that I decided to write.

In a nutshell, the research on women says this: Women are not the problem. The way we treat women is the problem. Women in our society face expectations and barriers that males do not. Whether at work, at home or in public, women are swimming in a sea of cultural rules that we inherited from our ancestors. And many of them are holding women back.

Although women know at a gut level that they face many obstacles, they do not know how to define them or to deal with them. And sadly, most women are so overworked they do not have the energy to turn their minds to the real things that are limiting their success.

About this Book

In *Lean Out* I shine a light on our corporate culture and the hidden systems that hold women back. I want women to see that it's not their fault they are not progressing as they had hoped. I want them to know that working harder or smarter will not actually lead to success, at least not in the long term, or it will likely come at a very high cost.

I think of this book as *the other half* of the best-selling book *Lean In* by Sheryl Sandberg. That book mostly urges women to change themselves by being tougher and more courageous if they want to get ahead. *Lean Out* urges both women (and men) to deal with our culture and shatters the thinking that women are mostly to blame for their lack of success. It shifts our focus to our systems, institutions and biases and shows how they are grossly unfair to more than half the population.

It is time to stop burdening women with the blame and responsibility for fixing an entire culture that treats women unfairly. It's time to tell the truth and truly allow women to be all they can be.

My Nightmare

Recently I had a dream about my research and it helped me understand why this book is so important. I dreamed that hundreds of women in all shapes and sizes, wearing brightly colored suits, were blindly walking off a steep cliff, one after another, to their deaths. It seemed to me that no one had told them that there was a cliff or had warned them about the potential dangers in the area. It was as if they had no clue. It reminded me of the joke we used to share in the workplace. When someone clearly offended the boss, we would say, "Didn't you get the memo?" as if we all knew what was really going on. Women are the 50% of the population that did not see what was happening to them because it was not obvious or predictable to them.

Lean Out is that memo – the one that women need and deserve.

A Final Note

This book is the result of my own perfect storm. It is a culmination of my entire life experiences that brought me to this particular point. If I had not practiced law for 20 years I could not have known how badly women are being treated. If I had not been a professor, I could not have conducted years of research, nor would I have had the credentials to have others pay attention. If I had not been a wife and mother I would not have known what women meant when they said they felt like slaves.

Indeed, I think it's fair to say that it took several university degrees, many years of law practice, teaching at two universities, authoring seven books, being a wife and raising two children to get me to the place where I could actually write this book. Not to mention my lifelong mission to end sexism and, of course, the thousands of mistakes I made, my many detours and my mindfulness practice. And most importantly, I wish to thank my husband, Mary-Jean Payeur, Catherine Leek, Karin Mizgala, Sandra Herd, Monica Beauregard, Mary Pappajohn, Christine Dearing, Denise Withers, Jennifer Leslie, Christine Unterthiner, Susanne Doyle-Ingram and Darrell Tomkins.

My dream is to have women and men as full partners in all aspects of life – at home, at work and in society. I really hope *Lean Out* makes a difference!

Introduction

"The blunt truth is that men still run the world." ~ Sheryl Sandberg

Have you ever wondered why men still run the world? Why do men hold about 80% of the most powerful positions in corporations and government? Why are there so many female college graduates yet so few women CEOs and politicians?

While women are integral participants in business and workplaces and are shown to be particularly effective as managers and entrepreneurs, they seem to disappear as we glance up the corporate and societal ladders. Catalyst, an international think tank that tracks women's progress, has repeatedly documented the significant benefits women contribute – from participation on corporate boards to customer service – all improving corporate performance, yet women are still absent in the highest positions of influence (see Appendix A: The Business Case for Advancing Women).

We think that women are advancing, but are they really? We think that women just need to work a bit harder to get those top positions and we just need a few more women in the pipeline in order to balance out the numbers.

But this is simply not true. Despite the promises of feminism, women today are by no stretch equal or powerful. Women continue to fall behind at work, at home and in society, and men are continuing to leap ahead. Men continue to hold the bulk of power while women are encouraged to take part-time work or stay at home and care for children, even though many have no option but to work.

In her best-selling book *Lean In,* Sheryl Sandberg, Facebook COO, beautifully describes the many barriers that hold women back and recounts the depressing statistics about women falling off corporate ladders. In her Preface Sandberg lists the obstacles women face, including "blatant and subtle sexism, discrimination and sexual harassment. Too few workplaces offer the flexibility and access to child care and parental leave that are necessary for pursuing a career while raising children. Men have an easier time finding mentors and sponsors who are invaluable for career progression. Plus women have to prove themselves to a far greater extent than men do."

Yet Sandberg chose to focus on women rather than institutional barriers. She urges women to be tougher, stronger and more courageous if they want to get ahead. As she says, "I am encouraging women to address the chicken [individual barriers] but I fully support those who are focusing on the egg [institutional barriers]." Like other women before her, she encourages women to work harder and "find balance" rather than focus on the corporate culture, systems, policies and our outdated ideas about women that prevent women from being truly powerful.

Unlike Sandberg, I do not ask women to become better climbers. I ask them to look at the ladder and question how it was built. Why is there a ladder at all and why is it so hard for women to climb? Why does it hold so many women back and yet propel so many men to the top?

Although self-help can be beneficial, history shows that this is not enough, and it may actually be causing the stagnation. As women go about "leaning in," the bigger and more resistant barriers facing women remain untouched. Not only do corporate institutions and policies flourish, but by continuing to call it a "women's issue" rather than a societal or corporate issue, we burden women with both the responsibility and burden of trying to make things better.

In their extensively researched book, *What Works for Women at Work*, Professor Joan C. Williams and Rachel Dempsey summarize and synthesize almost all of the academic research on this topic and conclude in no uncertain terms that the main reason women are not progressing is not because they are not working hard enough or there is something wrong with them. It is due to powerful biases and barriers.

Williams and Dempsey also ask women to work within the system but become more "politically savvy" in order to survive. They suggest things like: stand your ground (with softeners); laugh it off; get over yourself; present solutions, not problems; and manage your anger. Here is an example of their advice: "Angry women can trigger stereotypes of high powered females as ball-breakers or alternatively as hormonal nutcases – making it all the more important for women to remain in control of their anger rather than allowing it to control them."

In defense of taking a self-help approach, they state in their Conclusion, "This book has focused on what women can do for themselves because Joan decided that after working on institutional solutions for 15 years, organizations are changing so slowly that women need the tools now to navigate the world as they find it. But the real solution is to level the playing field."

As you will learn here, the real culprit is precisely the "playing field" that consists of our outdated mind-sets and the culture we inherited. Women suffer, not because they are incompetent, weak or lazy, but because we built a society and institutions that hold them back.

These are the things we never learned as we were growing up. Our mothers never told us, our teachers never told us, nor did our bosses or mentors. In this state of ignorance, we had no idea that we would become willing players, not just accepting but also promoting the status quo. This is a terrible shame.

It's time to stop blaming women and get to the heart of not just *how* women are being held back, but *why*. We need to learn to recognize the barriers but, just as importantly, understand why these barriers were constructed in the first place and why they are so hard to dismantle. We then need to work diligently on challenging each and every one of them if we truly want women to succeed.

Part One

We Can't See It Because It's Glass

Chapter 1

Admit There Is a Glass Ceiling

> "No doubt about it, the glass ceiling is alive and well. Nearly two thirds of the respondents in a *Los Angeles Times* poll of twelve thousand women reported experiencing sexual discrimination. Additionally, a survey released by the Society for Human Resource Management indicated nearly nine out of ten human resource professionals believe women face barriers to career advancement." ~ Susan Solovic

At a recent networking event, a young energetic woman in her 20s approached me. Beaming ear to ear she thrust her hand toward mine and shook it forcefully, saying, "It's so good to meet you Dr. Fitzgerald, I am looking forward to your presentation. However, I have to tell you that I don't believe there is any such thing as a glass ceiling."

Although my first impulse was to scream and shake this lovely being, I instead practiced a more peaceful technique of suspending judgment and replied, "So you haven't personally experienced the glass ceiling yet?" And to this she promptly said, "No, I have not experienced it, but I also do not believe it exists." In her opinion it did not serve her to look at the negative so she decided to ignore it. She said she did not see any point in whining and blaming others for her own failings. As she said, "If I focus on the negative it can only hold me back."

This story explains in a nutshell why the glass ceiling is so effective at holding women back. We think that the glass ceiling is a myth or "all in our heads." We decide that looking at it will serve no purpose and could potentially make things worse. We tell ourselves that "it's just the way things are" and we have to accept it. We assume that our corporate policies are fair and that women have finally achieved equality. We believe that if we simply work a bit smarter and harder we will avoid any pitfalls. And if by chance we hear about the daunting statistics on the slow progress of women, we convince ourselves that somehow these numbers don't relate to us personally. After all, we have our past successes to remind us that we are strong and resilient. We will persevere. That is how we dodge the bullet. And we can dodge it for a while.

Every year corporations and academics gather data and statistics about women's advancement. Year after year, the research shows that women are barely advancing at work and in business and in some cases are slipping back. Women hold significantly fewer numbers of powerful positions in corporations and government. Women are less likely than men to be considered for promotions and high-level positions. Women also earn less than men, are promoted less and have fewer mentors. The recent statistics below come out of the United States from the article, "The Women's Leadership Gap" (August 4, 2015) (see Appendix B). In the positions listed below, women account for the following percentages:

- Doctors   35.5%
- Movie directors of top 250 films   17%
- US House of Representatives   19.4%
- CEOs in S&P 500 US corporations   4.6%
- College professors (full)   30%

Every year, thousands of professional women find themselves unable to get past a certain point inside organizations. They stand by as men with similar credentials and experience get promotions and opportunities that they did not even know existed.

When women enter the work world, something dramatic happens to them. Confronted with hierarchies and male-based rules and practices, they begin the long journey of trying to fit in. Many do a brilliant job, at least for the first few years. They dress like men, talk like men and even smoke cigars like men. They pride themselves at succeeding in a man's world and thank the women's liberation movement for getting them this far.

At about 6-10 years into a working career, most women wake up and sense there is something wrong. The promotions start dwindling, the grind is still grinding and they begin to sense that they are doing something wrong or missing out. It's at this point that many women leave high-paying jobs to become entrepreneurs, often faring better outside the corporate world. Others volunteer and work out of their homes, while many brilliant and well-educated women become full-time caregivers and homemakers, earning no money at all. What we don't realize is that even though women were successful at getting in the door, there was no guarantee they would stay.

Catalyst, an American-based organization that tracks women's progress, discovered in 2010 that 68% of women believe that sex discrimination exists in the workplace. This includes over 60% of architects and almost 70% of female lawyers. Of women professionals in Washington D.C., 73% felt men had more opportunities than women.

Yet many women cannot see it. Susan Solovic explains why.

> Although women recognize on an intellectual level that discrimination is pervasive, they may not see it or choose to see it when it happens to them. This phenomenon is what I call the "gray-matter glass ceiling." It is a self-created, internal glass ceiling that you don't even know exists because it is part of who you are. Socialization, culture, demographics, religion, and gender stereotyping all contribute to your internal belief system and can result in your inability to see discrimination when it happens.

Whether we can see it or not, the so-called "glass ceiling" is alive and well. It consists of a combination of invisible factors that keep women from advancing. And by definition, it is glass and therefore invisible.

The most recent comprehensive academic book on the glass ceiling was written by mother and daughter, Professor Joan C. Williams and Rachel Dempsey in 2014. *What Works for Women at Work* is over 300 pages and contains hundreds of footnotes referring to decades of research on women at work. In their introduction they acknowledge that women are doing better than ever before and have made extraordinary strides in the professional world yet admit that "something's going wrong at the top."

As they say,

> The problem? As women get older, advance up the corporate ladder and begin to have families, their advantage not only disappears it turns into a striking handicap. As of 2011 only 3.6 percent of Fortune 500 CEOs were women – 16 white women, 2 women of color, 17 men of color and 465 white men. That's one table of women in a restaurant packed with 27 tables of men.

Williams and Dempsey point directly at four specific patterns of bias that hit women in mid-career. Women face pressure to prove themselves over and over and to walk a tightrope of double binds and higher standards than men. They also encounter competition and judging – often by other women. Most harmful, however, is the so-called "maternal wall" consisting of a host of obstacles that impact the advancement and income of mothers.

They also suggest that the reason the glass ceiling is so difficult to pin down is because it is often framed as a few small problems experienced by a handful of women. In reality, these individual experiences are part of a larger pattern or "accumulation of disadvantage," as described by Virginia Valain: "The well-meaning advice often given to women – not to make a mountain out of a molehill – is mistaken. That advice fails to recognize that mountains are molehills, piled one on top of the other."

The Bottom Line. Whether we like to admit it or not, the glass ceiling does exist. Although it may be invisible, we have clear data showing that women are not advancing at work or in business to the same extent as men. We think women have achieved equality yet women continue to be absent from the bulk of the higher offices and boardrooms inside corporations and are minor players in universities. Although we may think that the glass ceiling is an individual problem experienced by a few women, the fact that it impacts so many women suggests that something else is going on.

What To Do. We must pay close attention to research and look closely at the context in which we work. We must stop hiding our heads in the sand and shift our focus from individual women to the corporate ladder and the corporate playing field. By looking at the various factors that make up the glass ceiling we will come to better understand not just why women stall in mid-career but also why women leave corporations and, more importantly, what we need to do to ensure women stay and advance.

Chapter 2

Stop Telling Women to Lean In

"I'm a perfectly good carrot that everyone is trying to turn into a rose. As a carrot I have good color and a nice leafy top. When I'm carved into a rose, I turn brown and wither." ~ Mary Pipher

After practicing law for about 10 years I realized something significant about professional women that was different from men. I had always assumed that women were equal to men. I knew they were just as smart as men and most definitely worked just as hard. I assumed that if they did not succeed it was their own fault.

This idea was shattered at an event I attended a few years ago. "The Seven Deadly Career Mistakes Women Make" was presented to more than 200 professional women and it altered the course of my life. The speaker, a beautiful, tall, 30-something executive from a large recruiting firm, told us in no uncertain terms that women were seriously lagging behind.

The speaker told us that women have barely made headway into top positions in corporations and are rarely seen in influential or political positions. Women receive on average 75 cents for every dollar earned by men, they rarely advance at the same rate in careers as men and are not offered the same opportunities and mentoring as men. In other words, women lag behind men in terms of income, status and influence.

But rather than point to the real causes of these problems, she blamed women. According to her, there were seven main reasons we women were not succeeding in our careers. These included wearing the wrong clothes, not bragging enough, being too concerned about what others think and being too friendly.

Later that night I became deeply depressed and kept asking myself the same questions over and over: Why are there no talks like this for men? Why aren't men concerned about their mistakes? Why are women so much more concerned about getting ahead?

A slow, crushing wave of sadness crept over me as I began to imagine the hundreds, perhaps millions, of unbelievably talented and successful women who think there is something terribly wrong with them. These women, like me, somehow came to believe that we are *not quite good enough*. We think it is our fault for not getting ahead, for not asking for bigger raises and for not managing our workload and child care responsibilities better. And because we blame ourselves completely, we take on full responsibility for engaging in our own self-improvement no matter what the obstacles.

Then I had an "aha" moment.

What if the problem is not women? What if there is absolutely nothing wrong with women?

What if, instead, the problem is our thinking about women? What if the real problem is a world that cannot see women's true value? What if women are actually doing things correctly, but their bosses, their friends and their husbands are telling them that they are all wrong? What if we stopped asking women to improve themselves and instead asked everyone, as well as our institutions that reject women, to change. What if we embraced women and all their strengths?

Imagine that! Crazy talk, I know.

Most women think they are fundamentally flawed and entirely responsible for their slow success and advancement. This is no surprise since as a society we tell them day in and day out that they are not quite good enough. Women are not good enough to be CEOs or heads of countries and not good enough to be parents and professionals at the same time.

Every day in workplaces everywhere women are told that there is something wrong with them. We are told to be tougher, more courageous and less talkative. We are told that our speaking patterns are unfortunate and that the way we walk is troublesome. All of these things, we are told, are causing us to fail and must be remedied through self-improvement. Not only do we tell women they need to improve, we tell them they need to change in such significant ways that it's almost impossible.

This type of advice can be found in many business books written for women. Although these writers are well intended, they tend to suggest that women are doing many things wrong. In her bestselling book *Lean In*, Sheryl Sandberg urges women to be tougher, stronger and more courageous if they want to gain top leadership positions. In the best-selling books, N*ice Girl Don't Get the Corner Office* and *Women Don't Ask,* the authors suggest that many of the problems women encounter are due to their lack of assertiveness, particularly around asking for promotions and raises. This advice fails on two counts. It assumes that all women are passive or lacking in skills and it also fails to fully recognize (as discussed below) that women who take this advice are often perceived as too aggressive and suffer a backlash.

In their book *Womenomics,* Claire Shipman and Katty Kay tell women to either stay in lousy jobs or leave. Rather than challenging the status quo, these writers accept the world as it is and tell women that if they want to work in a man's world they must accept it and bend when necessary. Here is some of their advice:

- If the high-profile jobs you have been working on start drying up, just find a way to get back on the radar and keep that performance level high high high.

- If key decisions are made without you, don't get paranoid, maybe it's just that decisions are made on your day off so adjust your schedule.

- If someone less qualified is promoted over you, you need to either "re-calibrate" your expectations or speak to your boss about whether your contribution is still working for them!

This is the kind of advice that makes women feel like they are going crazy. It suggests that the treatment they are really experiencing is all in their heads. It denies their reality, but then tells them they just need to work harder. This advice undermines women and is not helpful.

We continually remind women directly and indirectly that they are not as good as men, particularly in leadership roles. Indeed, we often tell them that a woman's role is to support (from behind). So while urging them to lead, we also expect them to take notes, get coffee and work on volunteer committees. We also tell women if they change too much they will be called into question and be seen as frauds.

As a result of this propaganda, women engage in costly self-help, attending courses and reading books on perseverance, resilience and self-esteem. We come to believe that we just need a few more tips and strategies on being tougher and more ambitious. These beliefs, however, are not only turning women into workaholics, but are forcing them to engage in a continuous cycle of self-improvement.

The real kicker, however, is that this self-help rarely works in the long term. Although a few women succeed at getting to the top, many more live their lives under constant pressure to be different and better. Too many women feel as if they are pretending or acting much of the time and thus suffer a crisis in confidence. Many slog away never really feeling that they fit or are welcome. Caught in this bind, many women give up and leave workplaces sensing that the cost is simply too high.

The Bottom Line. We are told that the main reason women remain absent in the higher levels of corporations and government is because there is something wrong with them. We see them as not quite good enough and urge them to change and improve if they wish to be successful. We tell them to "lean in" and take responsibility for their own advancement. As a result, many women think they need to improve and engage in constant self-improvement, yet they never really achieve a lasting sense of success.

What To Do. We must stop telling women that there is something wrong with them. We must pull them off the treadmill of constant self-improvement and look at the context in which they work. Rather than telling women to improve, we need to look at the ways in which our corporate practices and outdated mind-sets make their lives so difficult. In other words, we must stop telling women to *lean in* and start asking men and women to *lean out* against the beliefs, systems and institutions that hinder women.

Chapter 3

Don't Fall for the Pipeline Theory

> "Corporate America is quick to point to the increased number of women in middle management positions as evidence that things are improving for women. To make the current state of affairs more palatable, an analogy is made of a pipeline that is supposedly filling up with capable and qualified women. Therefore, the story goes, it is only a matter of time before women reach equality in the boardrooms and executive suites.
> Yeah right. Talk about propaganda." ~ Susan Solovic

Most people think it's just a matter of time until women actually get the top positions in corporations, in politics and in society. They think there is a lack of qualified women in the world and that men get the top positions because there are no qualified women in sight.

They believe that as more women graduate from colleges and universities, the pool of competent women will grow and these women will eventually be selected for the top positions. In other words, more women in, more women up. According to this theory, women's slow progress has nothing to do with gender bias or discrimination; it's simply a matter of numbers. There are just not enough women in the system. And although it sounds good in theory, it's simply not true.

This so-called pipeline theory has been researched extensively by Catalyst. Several reports compare the number of college graduates to the number of successful women at the top and year after year they tell the same story. Females have been pouring into workplaces and graduating from colleges in equal numbers to men for more than 50 years. Although some women have found their way into mid-level management positions, they tend to stop there.

For example, female university professors struggle to attain tenure-track positions even though half the students in universities and colleges (more than half in some schools) are currently filled by women. Female academics tend to gravitate to low-paid and temporary research and teaching-assistant positions. As for lawyers, although half of law school graduates are women, studies involving thousands of lawyers with similar entry-level credentials have found that men are at least twice as likely as women to obtain partnership.

In her book *The Difference "Difference" Makes*, Law Professor Deborah Rhode looked at the data and concluded that the pipeline theory cannot explain the underrepresentation of women in leadership positions and, as she says, "the pipeline leaks and if we wait for time to correct this problem, we will be waiting a very long time."

Curiously, women and men see the pipeline very differently. When asked to explain why women are not in leadership positions, they provide strikingly different answers. According to Margaret Heffernan, in her book *The Naked Truth*, men think that the absence of women at the top is due to lack of experience. As she says, "This is patently absurd. Plenty of educated women are packing the pipeline. In the United States, women earn 57% of bachelor's degrees and 58% of master's degrees. We make up 46% of the workforce."

By focusing only on numbers, the pipeline theory fails to take into consideration some fairly obvious factors impacting women's career progress and, in particular, external, cultural and social factors. Specifically, Catalyst research uncovered the following reasons for the slow advancement of women:

- Women are not in positions that attract promotions (e.g., frontline workers and human resources);

- Women are left out of the informal corporate networking that leads to promotions;

- Women miss opportunities because they are not aware they are available;

- Women do not have mentors who watch their back and recommend them to others;

- Women face stereotypes about what women can and should do; and

- Work hours are not flexible to allow for other life commitments (e.g., flextime or part-time work).

In other words, although women make up more than half of the current workforce, they are promoted less and mentored less than men. They are offered fewer opportunities for growth and they still face institutional barriers such as stereotyping and discrimination.

Some corporations have recently tried to address this type of discrimination by adopting rigorous merit-based criteria for hiring and promoting employees. This type of meritocracy however has been called into question. Rather than being treated equally on the basis of merit, Joan C. Williams and Rachel Dempsey uncovered research that shows that those companies are actually more bias! This is apparently because people working within these systems trust the process, don't question the system and succumb more easily when bias does occur.

The reason we cling to the pipeline theory is because we actually want to believe that we are not bias and that we are not actually holding women back. Yet by falling for this myth we fail to notice the ever-enduring habits, corporate practices and ignorance that impact women negatively.

Indeed, not a week goes by that I don't see a well-intended powerful woman, like Carly Fiorina, past CEO of Hewlett-Packard, suggest that women are almost there. In 1999 when she was appointed, about 7% of the executives in the big tech companies were women. That means 93% were men.

> **Bottom Line:** Many of us think that the reason women are not advancing simply has to do with numbers. We think that there is a shortage of qualified women and that once more educated and skilled women get into the pipeline, women will achieve equality. Not only has this been disproven, but, by focusing only on numbers, we are blind to the other barriers that are holding women back.
>
> **What To Do.** We must stop falling for the pipeline theory. Instead we need to pay attention to the statistics that show that women are not advancing in spite of the number of graduates from colleges and universities. We must spend more time investigating what is really going on in workplaces and admit that other factors are at play that make up the glass ceiling, like discrimination, lack of mentoring and corporate culture.

Chapter 4

Ask Women Why They Really Leave

> "One reason more women aren't swarming the glass ceiling is that corporate business doesn't appeal to a huge number of females (only about 9 percent see it as their first-choice career). In addition, many women get disillusioned with corporate jobs and leave. Where do these women go? To start their own company! Almost half the businesses in the United States are owned by women." ~ Catherine Dee

In the prime of my career at age 42 after practicing law for 10 years, I was given the "big invisible squeeze" from my high-paying and exciting job. Like many other women, I returned from a very short maternity leave and found out that I was now reporting to two male bosses rather than one. My office was no longer next to the executive director but was now a former closet with no windows. My work responsibilities had changed significantly, and I was no longer working in my area of expertise.

I demanded an explanation and reminded my boss of my perfect attendance record and many accolades. I was told that although I was a very valuable employee, this was simply a matter of corporate restructuring and that (according to him) my skills were better suited to my new job. After all, I suffered no drop in pay. As for my office, I was reassured that they were working hard to find me a new office but would likely have to wait until the current lease expired in a year or so.

I spoke to the human resources person who said there was nothing she could do. It was a simple business decision. When I tried to I speak to my colleagues I was treated as if I had the plague. So much for camaraderie. I phoned an employment lawyer who told me that this was a very clear case of constructive dismissal and that I should ask for my former job back. He wrote a strong letter to my boss asking him to provide reasons for my demotion even though I knew my boss would likely hire a team of lawyers to write nasty and threatening letters to me. It should have been no surprise to me that I became so sick I could not work at all. When I phoned, my boss said, in a condescending tone, "Maybe it's best you stay home with your family." My body essentially forced me to give up a fight for my career and I eventually quit. They held a big party for me when I left, although no one could look me in the eye.

My story is not unique. My close friend Judy, a vice-president of an international hotel chain, has just been through 3 years of litigation for being squeezed out in a similar manner. In her case she refused to commit fraud so she was fired. Although she ultimately won her case in court, it came at a huge cost. She ended up having to mortgage her home to cover the legal fees and was an emotional basket case as she tried to raise her two daughters and fight this case. So much for the protection of the law.

There are hundreds or perhaps thousands of stories like these, in which women leave and never say a word. Each story is about a bright, ambitious, hard-working woman who one day found herself out of the workforce, too ashamed to tell anyone the truth. They blame themselves, often thinking that they must have done something terribly wrong and they feel a deep sense of shame and remorse. And because they feel so vulnerable and afraid that they might never get another job, they silently move along. I call it the "big invisible squeeze" or "death by a thousand small cuts."

In 2006 sociologist Louise Roth studied MBA graduates who began working in Wall Street securities firms in the 1900s. She found that about 40% of women left their jobs to find more balanced occupations while about the same number experienced some form of pregnancy discrimination. Roth suggests that when men leave jobs and say they want to spend time with their families, we all know it's a cover-up.

Researchers from Stanford found that top-performing women were not being honest in exit interviews because they wanted to maintain good relations with their former bosses. In one study the main reason women left was because, "they could not see a future for themselves there." As Leslie Bennetts says in *The Feminine Mistake,* "Either the women are unhappy with some aspect of their position or they got forced out. People just don't recognize it for what it is."

In their book, *Getting to 50/50*, Sharon Meers and Joanna Strober include an entire chapter titled, "Women Don't Quit Because They Want To." They refer to several studies describing the real reasons women leave paid work. In one study of professional women who quit their jobs to say home only 16% felt the decision was relatively unconstrained. Most women said their husband was the primary reason for their decision. This included his work hours, his lack of participation in child and home care, his desire to have a wife at home and his ability to support the family. The other main factor was the amount, pace and inflexibility of work in today's 24/7 world. Another study by Korn/Ferry found that the main motivator to leave was "desire for opportunity."

Pamela Stone, author of *Opting Out?,* found that two-thirds of the women she interviewed tried to adjust their schedules so that they could accommodate family responsibilities. She also found that unlike the myth of "maternal pull," the decision by these women was a, "deliberate and thoughtful, long and protracted, complex and, except for the women who had always intended to stay at home, difficult and doubt-filled."

As we look closer we begin to see that women aren't voluntarily leaving great jobs – they are being driven out. Here are some of the myths about why women leave and the more likely truths.

Myth	The More Likely Truth
She just can't take it.	The workplace is not conducive to growth as a human.
She wants to be with her kids.	She can make more money as an entrepreneur.
She isn't a team player.	She does not have a mentor or colleagues who support her.
She has family obligations.	She can't find quality, affordable child care.
She is not a big rainmaker.	She has few networks and is not included in the boys' club.
She does not play the game.	She does not want to waste her time on office politics.
She throws her weight around.	When she speaks up, she is seen as too aggressive.
She does not have the balls.	When she shows emotions, she is seen as weak.
She is a bitch.	She is criticized for simply being assertive.
She cares too much.	She likes to listen to people and create win/win situations.
She burns bridges.	She is rarely given a second chance.

In her book, *The Naked Truth,* Margaret Heffernan explains how these myths form much of the corporate culture that makes workplaces hostile for women. We like to blame women, yet when asked to name the most significant roadblocks to their advancement women cited cultural barriers and specifically, "male stereotyping and preconceptions of women" and "exclusion from informal networks of communication" as the top two. Another near the top was "inhospitable corporate culture."

As Heffernan says, "Companies that tolerate, endorse, or even encourage exclusive behavior by men are hostile environments for women. This doesn't mean that they are impossible to work in – but it does mean that we aren't welcome and we will find it hard to build support of the kind that every career needs."

Exclusion of women is often hidden in one small word: fit. Women just don't fit. Indeed, research conducted on group behavior shows that those within a particular group are more likely to include those who are similar. In other words, it is human nature that people tend to like the people who are like themselves. And men like themselves, so women are often excluded or expected to assimilate.

Heffernan describes it this way:

> When women first got into business, we knew we'd have to work hard not to disrupt the status quo. As gatecrashers, we were so eager to get in that we agreed to be good girls, behave, not rock the boat. We did that by conforming to roles that made *them* feel comfortable. At first, this took the shape of severe women in stout shoes and ruthlessly tied-back hair: by being totally sexless and quasi-military...we were absorbing lessons about how to behave in ways that would not aggravate or threaten men. Like new immigrants, we assimilated in order not to be thrown out.

The Bottom Line: Although we like to believe the myth that women have achieved equality and women are leaving because they prefer less stressful work or wish to care for children, the research says otherwise. Many women leave high-paying careers, not because they find the work too difficult but because of the working conditions and many other quite practical factors. Just like men, they leave for better opportunities and advancement. They also leave because of lack of flexibility, lack of camaraderie, exclusion and lack of fit. They often search for options before leaving and rarely leave without serious consideration. Others feel the combined pressures and rather than freely opt out suffer the "big invisible squeeze" or "death by a thousand cuts" and leave on a sour note.

What To Do: We must first stop lying about why women leave. Knowing that women are afraid to tell the whole truth on departure from a job, it is important to gather solid information so that we can better understand how the combination of circumstances caused them to leave. Second, we must really listen to women when they remain at work. Their concerns must be taken seriously. So when a woman says something like, "I feel like I don't belong," don't assume that she is a recluse. Armed with this information we can create workplaces that are better suited for women.

Chapter 5

Notice the Absurd Expectations We Place on Women

> "Society teaches women, as young girls, not to be bossy, too aggressive, or a 'know it all.' Did you ever have a bossy friend in your play group or in your class at school? She probably didn't have a lot of friends because no one liked the way she bossed everyone around. Girls are taught to share, take turns, and play nicely together. In the business world, we try to preserve the inclusive cooperative nature of our play groups. Because we don't want to be perceived as being too bossy, we phrase things in a less threatening, nondirect manner. Unfortunately, it is not only less threatening but demeaning and signals a lack of self-esteem." ~ Susan Solovic

I have always been surprised at how many of my female lawyer friends are willing to work twice as hard as their male colleagues to get ahead. They volunteer for the non-paying committee jobs and work overtime well into the night. And because the "normal" work hours of a typical law firm are already completely absurd, these women turn into complete workaholics and neurotics. Then worst of all, this becomes the standard for the new female lawyers.

Sadly, most women accept this absurdity as the cost of a professional woman's career. They fall for the lie that if you want to be really successful, you must sacrifice everything for the firm. Because men face similar expectations, women think it's all fair. After all, they have the choice to leave at any time. And leave they do.

Women are expected to have the highest marks, the most degrees, the most relevant experience and are expected to be completely dedicated and loyal to the corporation or firm. Then, to add icing to the cake, women are expected to be kind, sympathetic, considerate, generous, caring and friendly – to absolutely everyone. And if women want to reach the top they must also be tough, strong and even cut-throat. Women are not only told that they must be perfect but that they must *work twice as hard* as men to even be noticed.

What women do not see is the particular cost to them as females and the pressures that are specific to them being women. They do not realize that the bar is not only different but much higher for them. They cannot see that the astonishing pressures and expectations they face are also inconsistent with who they have been taught to be and opposite to what they know intrinsically as females.

From the time we were little girls, we were fed very specific cultural messages about what we can do and who we should be as females. From grandma to television, females are told to be quiet and calm, to be nice to everyone and never show outward anger, particularly at another person. Even to this day girls are told to be "sugar and spice and everything nice."

One of the most restrictive cultural expectations shows up as double standards. This means that we label certain behaviors as good when males do them, but bad when females do them. The exact same behaviors are slotted into a gender category so women and men learn very quickly that boys and girls will be perceived very differently even when doing the exact same thing. Here are a few examples from the book *He's a Stud, She's a Slut* by Jessica Valenti:

- He's neat. She's neurotic.
- He's angry. She's PMSing.
- He's childless. She's selfish.
- He's a player. She's a ho.
- He's a bachelor. She's a spinster.

These messages and thousands more are reinforced constantly in our culture via families, television, the Internet and magazines. Families reduce women to unpaid labor, television stereotypes women and the Internet sexualizes women. Magazines are filled with images of scantily dressed women in vulnerable poses, reinforcing the idea that women are not to be taken seriously. Even business magazines barely mention women. All of these cultural messages suggests that women aren't really that powerful, not very important and do not really belong in positions of leadership, power or influence.

> **The Bottom Line.** Most of us do not notice the absurd pressures and expectations that professional women face. Women are expected to be brilliant and hard-working, to be kind and likeable (by everyone), to volunteer lots and to be completely loyal and dedicated to the firm or corporation. But this is not all. They must also be attractive, perfect and walk a tightrope of double standards. This perfection pressure takes a toll on women's health and relationships, and although some women succeed at work, many fall off the path along the way.
>
> **What To Do.** We must pay more attention to the kinds of pressures we place on women and begin to challenge them. Although the next section of this book is dedicated to this topic, a quick way to learn about gender-based expectations is to watch, *Killing Us Softly*, a documentary based on lectures by Jean Kilbourne. It shows how media pressures girls and women to be sexy, small and passive. It is my favorite video on gender. By watching the images and photographs you will come to understand how the media reinforces our society's expectations of women, by promoting stereotypes and sexualizing women and girls, usually without us even noticing.

Part Two

There Is Nothing Wrong with You

Chapter 6

Question the Tightrope of Double Binds

> "To get ahead, women must not simply demonstrate that they are qualified; they must be better qualified and willing to work harder than men. It is much like being guilty until proven innocent. Men, on the other hand, are automatically assumed to be competent until proven otherwise – and sometimes not even then." ~ Susan Solovic

A few years ago I was walking back to my Toronto law office with a client, when he gave me a huge compliment. I had just won a case defending his manufacturing business and he told me how great it was to work with me. He said I was an exceptional lawyer, really listened and was both direct and considerate in my approach. I was deeply flattered since it was my aim to balance the harsh adversarial climate with a compassionate approach. But then he said something that I have never forgotten. He said, "The whole process was amazing. You were amazing. I just wish you had pounded your fist on the table a few times to show them who's boss." Although I laughed at the time, the words stuck with me, even to this day.

Almost every professional woman has faced the assertive/aggressive double bind. We tell women that pounding fists and being aggressive is both necessary and effective, yet we have trained them all their lives to never show any sort of hostile emotions. We ask women to be more *cutthroat* but abhor the slightest violence perpetrated by females. We are told to be tough but not too threatening, outspoken but not too opinionated. We tell women to play hardball but not hurt feelings or "burn bridges."

Women struggle with these types of expectations day in and day out. These are just a few of the tightropes or "double binds" that professional women face. They force us into no-win or Catch-22 situations.

As most women know, if they act too much like men they will be rejected for being aggressive or pushy yet if they do not act assertively enough they will be seen as spineless or simply invisible. If they act too much like women they will be ignored but if they do not act feminine enough they will be called bitches. This double bind comes in many forms. For example, women must be:

- Tough but not a ball breaker;
- The boss but not bossy;
- Career-oriented but not ambitious;
- Powerful but not more powerful than men;
- Individual but also inclusive;
- A leader, but preferably from behind;
- Ambitious but not a braggart;
- Nice but not too touchy-feely;
- Attractive but not too sexy; and
- Friendly but not "chatty Cathy."

In simple terms these double binds tell women that they should act as masculine as possible without going over the fine line that makes them look like a man (i.e., strong and powerful) and at the same time act feminine but not so far as to be seen as a woman (i.e., weak and ineffectual).

If you look closer, you may notice that many of the "double binds" involve males telling females to do things "their way" based on their own male-based personal experience. This causes several problems.

First, the double binds assume that the masculine way is the ideal way to work and that it actually works best. It suggests that women who show masculine characteristics are most effective and efficient. Yet most people know that things like aggression can work on occasion but not all the time.

Second, it assumes that women have the ability to be more masculine and can do so in an instant. We assume that women have both the knowledge and the skills to act in a masculine manner. Yet as most people know, only a few women are truly effective at this (think Margaret Thatcher). As well, girls are shunned for using their masculine strengths, like a loud voice or physical strength. Beginning in early childhood, girls learn what it means to be a girl: nice, quiet and obedient. Males, on the other hand, not only learn early how to be aggressive and competitive but are encouraged to be so. In fact most men are not only proficient at the masculine skills, they have had many opportunities to practice them and thus enjoy using them.

Third, these double binds assume that women actually *want* to act this way and desire to be more masculine. I seriously doubt this to be true.

Here is the real catch. There is no one "right" way for a woman (or a man) to behave. Most workplace situations command that we become chameleons. A woman will be perceived as direct in one situation but pushy in another and so on. The tightrope is different for every single situation and so the amount of effort and skill required becomes overwhelming. To adhere to these double binds would make anyone completely neurotic. There is no winning.

The real cost of walking this tightrope comes at the loss of the feminine. In an attempt to act in this way, women forget there is a feminine approach that might be more effective or efficient. They sacrifice their true feminine strengths and powerful abilities like sensing and intuition.

The irony is that women somehow believe that acting masculine will give them access to the masculine world of power, status and influence but, as noted in other parts of this book, this rarely happens. Sadly, most professional women have been *acting* their whole lives, trying to be something they are not and may never be.

> **The Bottom Line.** Women face a tightrope of double binds or no-win expectations. We are told to be assertive but not aggressive; to be the boss but not bossy; to be pretty but not sexy. We are expected to be tough, but not too tough; direct but not too direct; powerful but not too powerful; feminine but not too feminine. In effect, women are told: Do not act like a (weak) woman and do not act like a (strong) man. Not only is this profoundly confusing, but to walk this fine line is a full-time job and ultimately impossible. Not only that, but women are told to reject the very strengths they have perfected over their lives and their feminine intelligence.
>
> **What To Do.** We must notice the torturous double binds we place on professional women and question them. Why do you think we expect women to be assertive but not aggressive? This is not as simple as it sounds because these double binds are rooted in the basic assumption that the male-based way is the best and only way to do things. And sadly we see the feminine as weak or bad. We must question the masculine and elevate the feminine at the same time if we want to tap the best of both. We must stop making women continually feel bad about themselves for not being able to walk this ridiculous tightrope every day. In an ideal world we can honor both masculine and feminine approaches.

Chapter 7

Don't Expect Women to Be Mini-Men

> "Therefore, to become a more effective communicator, you must begin by opening your mind and exploring the subtleties, nuances, and preferences of a foreign culture, the male culture, as if you were preparing to do business in a foreign country." ~ Susan Solovic

There is a well-known inspirational speaker whose famous advice to women launched him into fame a few years ago. The title of his talk was: "What Women do Wrong in Business." I went to hear him speak to a group of women lawyers and was surprised that he was in his early 20s. Although he had not attended college, he told us that he had *years* of experience as an entrepreneur.

He said he was bothered and dismayed by what he saw happening to women in business deals. Women were failing badly and obviously had no idea how men conducted business. As a result, women kept making huge mistakes and men were apparently running circles around us and taking full advantage. Women stumbled in negotiations, left money on the table and were failing to secure big business contracts. He told us that men did not view us as tough enough or serious enough and that we were sabotaging ourselves and other women.

His solution was to convince us all to start behaving more like men. He told us to speak louder and more assertively, stop trying to be liked and to be a bit more *cut-throat*. Sadly, I watched as women lined up to sign up for his executive coaching program hoping to find out what it really takes to succeed in a man's world.

I did not join them because I had already spent 15 years following this exact advice. I knew very well that not only did his strategy not work; it caused women to sell their souls to a system that also did not work. I was confident that one day most of these women would realize that they had been duped, hopefully sooner rather than later.

For my entire career as a lawyer, mediator and professor I was told to act more like a man. Although I was rarely told this directly, I was often pulled aside by well-meaning colleagues who told me that in order to be liked and to fit in better I should do things like:

- Try to avoid pink, yellow or "soft" colors.
- Wear "power" suits, preferably navy or black.
- Wear buttoned-up collars, never open-neck blouses.
- Don't show legs or cleavage.
- High heels were distracting.

There are hundreds of books that tell women that they must behave more like men if they want to be truly successful. Although it might not be obvious from a title, most books for executive women try to convince them that they all need to start looking, acting and even thinking like a man. Like Henry Higgins in the film *My Fair Lady*, they ask, "Why can't a woman be more like a man?"

Lean In is the most recent example. Although Sheryl Sandberg single-handedly created a modern women's movement she, like others, asks women to not only be more masculine but also to play within the man's game. This pressure is not only problematic on an individual level but by behaving like men, women participate in reinforcing the status quo and thus forget to question this culture at a fundamental level.

In her book Sandberg discusses the institutional barriers, but decides it is more important to help women on a personal level by encouraging them to work on their "internal barriers" by building self-confidence and courage; to "lean in" instead of pulling back. She states: "My argument is that getting rid of these *internal* barriers is critical to gaining power. Others have argued that the women can get to the top only when the *institutional* barriers are gone."

Although I agree that both approaches are necessary, they are most definitely not of equal importance. I do not agree that women should continue to twist themselves in knots to be more masculine and make personal sacrifices to fit into a brutal work world. I do not agree that women should exert energy to spend time on *both* fronts – self and institutions.

However, I do know that women feel a whole lot better when making personal change. We feel in control when we believe change is within our power. We buy self-help books and we get busy on our few minor adjustments. What we don't realize is that it is just as easy to deal with institutional barriers if we know how. And the impact of these changes is not limited to our personal sphere, but impacts many women over a more sustained period of time.

As I read *Lean In*, I was reminded of Gail Evans, the CNN executive who wrote a similar book in the late 1990s. She also advised professional women to be tougher and manlier. Luckily she realized her mistake and wrote a follow-up book years later titled *She Wins, You Win,* admitting that her first book was wrong and that women needed to address the hidden systemic barriers in order to truly succeed.

The sad truth is that asking women to behave more like men can actually help them – at least in the short term. Many women actually get into higher-level positions. Some actually think they are being treated fairly or at least like their male colleagues. Others, however, suffer a deep crisis in confidence, wondering why they can't seem to fit in. Many lose a chunk of their self-esteem and allow their feminine aspects to atrophy. Too many find it's just too damned hard to grow a penis and leave a whole lot poorer.

But it's not just the women who suffer. Our institutions suffer from narrow-sightedness and do not have the benefit of diversity and creativity. Too many organizations suffer high turnover and lose valuable women, yet wonder what they are doing wrong. Why don't women stay? Why can't we recruit more women? The very women who leave are the ones who might have been able to challenge the very structures that caused them to leave in the first place.

> **The Bottom Line.** We continuously tell professional women that if they want to succeed in a man's world, they must look, think and act like men. We must walk taller, speak louder and be more assertive. We must be more logical and direct. We promote women who look and act masculine and those who don't succeed are told that they don't have what it takes.
>
> Although this seems to makes sense in the short term, the long-term cost is way too high, not just to women but to our whole society. Women feel inadequate and sell their souls to a masculine culture. In doing so they sacrifice their deepest feminine strengths and spend too much time trying to be something they can never be. By focusing on making women better we lose sight of the institutional barriers allowing sterile cultures to flourish.
>
> **What To Do.** We must stop telling women they must act more like men. We must stop expecting them to wear suits and hide their feminine side. We must stop telling them there is something wrong with them if they cry, show empathy or value relationships. We must look at our corporate playing field and question why masculine attributes and characteristics are so highly valued. Why do we encourage aggression and downplay sensitivity? Maybe it's not women who need to act more like men but rather men who need to act more like women.

Chapter 8

Question Why Women Need More Courage

> "A male executive once counseled me to be less direct and assertive because he found that my style offended people. When I asked if he would make the comment to me if I were a man, he admitted that he would not. Therefore, I told him that I considered his comment a compliment." ~ Susan Solovic

It drives me crazy when someone says to a woman, "What's wrong with you? Why didn't you stand up for yourself!? Why didn't you negotiate harder? Where is your backbone? Have you no courage?"

Have you ever noticed how often we tell women that they just need a bit more courage or confidence? Indeed Sheryl Sandberg, in her book *Lean In*, tells women that they lack courage and confidence and without it, they will never be truly successful. She also suggests many practical solutions, such as raising our hands more and negotiating harder, all of which sound awfully sensible and familiar, yet don't feel quite right.

At the core of all these suggestions is the belief that women simply need to shift their thinking. They just need to think about themselves in a more positive way and that this in turn (and this alone) will result in more behaviors that will lead to success. It is much like cognitive behavioral therapy (CBT) or replacing negative thoughts with more positive ones.

Indeed, almost every self-help book for women suggests that it is women's thinking that gets them into trouble. One book title describes it all: *How to Change the Patterns of Thinking that Block*

Women's Paths to Power. The solution according to many authors is to teach women how to stop being so negative and self-critical and adopt behaviors that reflect confidence rather than low self-esteem.

This makes abundant sense. Simply stop putting yourself down and downplaying your abilities or else people will walk all over you. Promote yourself more, broadcast your accomplishments and talents and be outwardly proud (in a modest kind of way). You simply need to start by replacing your negative thinking and self-effacing actions with more positive thinking and assertive behaviors and doors will open for you.

We follow this advice because we know from experience that when we speak more firmly and stand taller, we are not only more likely to be noticed but by doing so we actually feel stronger and more authoritative.

We are also told that many traditionally feminine behaviors are problematic and can impede women's progress in the workplace. This is because they signal deference and subordination. Such behaviors include casting our eyes downward, lowering our voices and making our bodies small. Although most women know at some level that these actions are perceived as weak, we also know that these are the behaviors generally expected of women.

So before we abandon all our "negative thinking" and "inappropriate behavior" it is useful to step back, look at the bigger picture and notice the full impact of what is being suggested. Although these comments look like good practical advice, they may not be entirely effective and may even set women back. Here is how this advice often plays out with women who wish to gain confidence.

Stage 1: First we tell a woman that she needs a bit more courage and must act more assertively. So she signs up for a course and reads a few books on self-esteem and assertiveness. She learns how to employ strategies like positive thinking, affirmations, reality checking and speaking up. She learns how to be "firm but kind" particularly when negotiating for promotions and raises. As a result, she feels empowered.

Stage 2: When this woman takes her newly found skills and confidence back to the office, she begins to feel pushback. Colleagues no longer like her; men in particular avoid her and tell her that she has lost her sense of humor. She stops getting invited to lunches and meetings. The secretaries start calling her a bitch boss behind her back. She is eventually told by her supervisor that she is too tough and that a more gentle approach might work.

Stage 3: So she retreats and blames herself. She hires a business coach to teach her the fine art of being a strong woman in power. The coach (usually a masculine woman) shows her how to lead from behind, how to stop offending men by appearing too strong, how to be both firm but never pushy and do things like give credit to your boss for your work. And above all else, never show cleavage and always smile.

Stage 4: The woman works day in and day out trying to master these very delicate, difficult and often self-contorting tasks. Usually she feels like a fraud or chameleon. People pick up on this and see her as inauthentic and untrustworthy. She becomes an outcast, gets rejected, loses her self-confidence and decides to lie low, below the radar of attacks. Eventually some new boss notices her amazing potential and wonders why she has so little courage. He tells her to get some! And the cycle continues.

As you can see, positive thinking and positive acting only get you so far and may even backfire.

More importantly, however, something is overlooked. This is the fact that most women do not actually need more courage or confidence at all. Indeed research shows that women are just as assertive as men in different situations (think of a mother disciplining her child).

As Joan C. Williams and Rachel Dempsey discovered, "While women are often exhorted just to speak up, this reluctance may be tied to a woman's quite realistic sense of having more to lose than a man might in a similar situation." This is demonstrated in research that shows that women's deferential speech patterns (like "I am not sure if this is right but...) disappear when women are in all-women settings.

As most women know, when men are overly assertive we see them as odd or amusing but when women act in this way, we see them in quite negative terms, like a bitch. Not only that, but as Williams and Dempsey noticed, "Women who achieve success in the workplace face social rejection, taking the form of dislike and personal derogation. This kind of backlash not only can hurt women socially but can also negatively impact women's evaluations and their chances for raises or promotions."

For example, in a study of people participating in an executive training program, women negotiated less for their own salary than they did for others. This research suggests that women are likely aware of the cost to them personally of self-promotion. Research also shows that women tend to downplay their abilities and hesitate before taking on risky tasks until totally qualified. In a fresh light these behaviors appear more indicative of avoiding possible risks of overselling oneself or appearing arrogant. In other words, lack of courage looks more like a risk aversion strategy.

Williams and Dempsey explain it this way. "Most advice books scorn women soundly for this behavior. But what women are doing is a rational response to gender bias: men are more willing to take risks because doing so is less risky."

As we look more closely and gain a better understanding of women within our cultural settings, we quickly come to the conclusion that women are masters at relationships and assessing complex interpersonal situations. Indeed many women who do rise to the top are good at playing "the game," otherwise they get shoved out.

When women state assertions as if they were questions, they are doing so to avoid making others feel stupid. They offer their brilliant ideas as if they were just randomly contemplated to allow others to feel part of the process. They say things like, "That's a great idea, Bob," knowing they mentioned it to Bob last week.

Women have learned all their lives exactly how to behave to get things done, and walk that fine line of being strong but not so strong that they raise red flags. From the day they are born, girls learn who has the power and how to use their somewhat limited power to persuade others to listen and follow. They are not stupid. They learn very quickly what to say and when to say it. They learn early on that it is inappropriate to seek or wield power, particularly in relation to boys or men. They learn not to yell, learn not to be seen as too pushy or bossy and never get physical. They learn how to include everyone, to like everyone and also to put others first.

As a result many women learn precisely when they have the power to push and when they do not. They eventually learn the exact point at which they will be perceived as too aggressive. And even more importantly, women know the high cost if they don't get it right. If women speak too loudly they will not be invited out to lunch. If they embarrass a man in public, they will never get a promotion again.

Many women have told me of situations where they inadvertently "burned bridges" or damaged relationships with men so badly, they could never be repaired. Yet men often trash relationships with other men with apparently little impact. To men it's all part of the game – you win some, you lose some. To women, losing is simply too costly and must be weighed out carefully or avoided. And because so few women succeed, we have come to know that we are very lucky if we can dance this dance without being tossed off the dance floor for stepping on someone's toes. All of this explains why so many women do not want to take risks and do not want to raise their hands.

In an ironic way it may be that the women who actually succeed in business are the very ones who actually have (or at least show) less courage or are not concerned about asserting their power. Whether naively or with disinterest they stay silent, don't rock the boat and voila – they get promoted. If this is true, then perhaps we should be telling women to reduce their level of courage and stop putting their hands up!

> **The Bottom Line.** Many people think that the reason women are not progressing is because they don't have enough courage or confidence. We think that women suffer from negative thinking that can be remedied by positive thinking. We tell them to shift negative thoughts, raise their self-esteem and learn how to be assertive and they will be successful. Unfortunately this advice does not always work and often backfires. More importantly this advice is a misdiagnosis of what is really happening. Most women do not lack courage at all. Instead they are demonstrating highly sophisticated risk-aversion strategies. Women are masters of relationships and know all too well just how easily they can be knocked out of the game and just how hard it is to get back in and they act accordingly.
>
> **What To Do.** Stop asking women to be more courageous and look instead at the context in which they work. It's okay to suggest women adopt positive thought patterns but also acknowledge that assertive behaviors can actually backfire for women. We need to understand the roots of women's submissive behavior and create cultures where women will not be criticized for being strong. This involves offering women many chances and standing behind them when doing something risky. Don't crucify women for making mistakes. The so-called lack of confidence and self-esteem can only be cured by accepting women for their true strengths and creating environments where they can flourish.

Chapter 9

Reject Outdated Stereotypes

> "Gender bias is insidious. It transforms itself though varying disguises, taking on different shapes and sizes, and it affects every one of us at some point in our careers. Still think it hasn't happened to you? Stop for a minute and think about the number of times that you were in a meeting with a group of men and they expected you to keep the meeting notes." ~ Susan Solovic

Imagine you are sitting in a boardroom with about ten male top-level managers. While waiting for the CEO to arrive, a tall woman walks in. You notice her and do a quick scan. First you notice her height, and then her hair — is it long, short, pulled back? You will sense her demeanor, how she carries herself and whether she is smiling or not. Then you will notice her outfit, the shape and cut. You will notice if she is wearing a dress or skirt, since these are rare in boardrooms. You will likely look at her legs and notice her high heels. Just like everyone else in the room, you will have summed this woman up in about 10 seconds.

Armed with these visuals, your brain will start manufacturing assumptions about her. She will be labeled as either important or not. A secretary or an executive. Someone you want to get to know, or someone you can ignore. But unfortunately these assumptions, unlike your direct observation of her physical presence, are usually wrong.

This is because we are all biased. We sum up her position, her personality, her education level and her competence before she even speaks a word. This human tendency to judge and make assumptions, which is based only on our unique personal experiences, is very powerful. It can get us in all sorts of trouble and it also holds women back. These thought patterns are called prejudice (pre-judging), sexism and discrimination.

In the late 1990s a group of social scientists created a tool to measure our unconscious biases. This Implicit Association Test (IAT) has been used for many years and helps uncover our hidden thoughts about such concepts as women. The most astounding aspect of the research shows not just that we all hold biases but that we actually think we do not. Indeed many people vigorously suggest that they are neutral when this is not reflected in the test results. This may show how uncomfortable we are about having to admit our biases but also might explain why it is so difficult to change these assumptions.

Most people I meet have no idea about the ways in which we judge women. In fact most people deny adamantly that they treat women differently. Yet research paints a very different picture. According to Susan Solovic in her book *The Girls' Guide to Power and Success*, 61% of women executives say they have been mistaken for a secretary at a business meeting. We harbor so many assumptions about women and girls that it is shocking.

Many studies show that in job interview settings a male will often be preferred over a female with the same qualifications. The most well know research is from Stanford and is called the "Howard and Heidi" research. Students were given identical resumes with different names on the top: either Heidi Rosen or Howard Rosen at random. The results showed that although the students saw the two candidates as equally competent and accomplished, Heidi was seen as more selfish and therefore less of a candidate.

Here is a quick exercise to help you uncover your implicit bias about females. Look at each of the following words for 30 seconds at a time: GIRL. LADY. MOTHER. WIFE. SISTER. WOMAN. FEMALE. Now visualize a picture in your mind of what each word represents. For example the word "girl" might conjure up a room full of 5-year-old girls in a playground. The word "lady" might conjure up an old woman in a rocking chair. Once you have fairly clear pictures in your mind, you can begin to understand how these pictures reflect your hidden assumptions and how each time you use a word it attracts a whole bundle of assumptions.

At a very fundamental level, many of us still think that females are the weaker sex. We think women are not very strong, physically or emotionally, and are prone to irrational thoughts and mood swings. Many of us believe that females are flighty, confused and often unfocused. We do not think that women are competent at dealing with complex issues or leading companies or governments. We still think that females are better at childrearing, domestic work and cooking, and that they even enjoy it. Although these things might be true about some women, when we apply them to all women, they are called biases.

Academics refer to this bundle of assumptions, which are passed along from generation to generation, as the *femininity message*. They are the messages we give girls and women about what it means to be feminine and they define what females can and cannot do. Unfortunately they are at the root of many of our female stereotypes. Psychologist Sidra Stone's research uncovered three fairly narrow yet enduring stereotypes that we tend to squeeze women into:

- *Bitches:* These women are successful in the world of men. We tend to not view them as fully functioning women and are often waiting for them to stop being frauds (and fall in love with a man).

- *Mothers:* These women accept the protection of men and stay in the home, out of public life. We view them as large-breasted and nurturing but weak. Their role is only to raise kids and do housework.

- *Sages:* These women reject the rules and remove themselves from the game. These include concubines, witches and wise women crones.

These are just three of our gender stereotypes. As you can see, they are all based on outdated, preconceived notions about women. The way in which we pressure women to fit into these roles is by imposing on them certain expectations. Here are some of the most common cultural messages that women hear on a daily basis. When looking at the list, ask yourself the extent to which males face similar expectations.

- If you are loud or funny, you will be called obnoxious.
- If you are too smart, you will be rejected for being brainy.
- If you stand up for yourself, you will be called selfish.
- If you are not agreeable, you will be labeled as bitchy.
- If you protest openly, you will be called radical or delinquent.
- If you brag, people take you down saying: "Who does she think she is?"
- If you are athletic and like sports, you must be butch or gay.
- If you are not attractive, you must be lonely and all alone.
- If you are too strong, you will be called a tomboy.
- If you are messy or don't dress neatly, you will be regarded with disdain.
- If you aren't perfect, no one will notice you or care about you.

One of the harshest stereotypes that professional women face is that of mother. The minute a woman announces her pregnancy, she is treated completely different by almost everyone. No man suffers the same judging when he becomes a father. The two main inaccurate assumptions are that mothers are frail and in need of special treatment and that mothers are devoted to their baby and thus no longer able to commit to work. Although women have been devoting their lives to their careers for decades, there continues to be a prejudice that assumes moms are less serious about their careers because of their domestic responsibilities.

Even worse, in her research, sociologist Louise Roth discovered that many women faced discrimination as *both* mothers and potential mothers (i.e., all women under 40). Both were considered negative even though her research shows that being a mother, like being a father, is irrelevant to the level of commitment of a job. Like fathers, mothers flourish in business and at work.

> **The Bottom Line.** We all pre-judge women, whether we like to admit it or not. We make grand sweeping assumptions simply because they are female and then treat them differently on the basis of this bias. We assume that females are the weaker sex and are not very physically or emotionally strong. We think they are flighty and scattered, prone to irrational thoughts and overly sensitive. We squeeze them into outdated stereotypes and convince ourselves that they do not have the competence or commitment to be in high-level positions. If they are mothers they face blatant discrimination. And because these outdated beliefs are buried deep in our subconscious, we do not even realize they are playing out and holding women back as a result.

What To Do. We must take responsibility for our own biases and assumptions about females. Every single person should look at his or her own beliefs critically and challenge those that are holding women back. This is not easy, since they are invisible and mostly unconscious. One of the best places to start is by reading books and watching educational videos on discrimination and diversity. By doing so we can better understand how our society, media and families pass along outdated beliefs about males and females. A good place to start is by measuring your implicit bias regarding women at this Harvard website: https://implicit.harvard.edu/implicit/.

Chapter 10

Stop Asking Women to Speak Louder

> "The deeper male voice, we are taught, is the one voice that conveys authority. When women in television commercials are pictured scrubbing, rubbing, and tubbing, a male voice off-camera will do the sales pitch. If a male voice did not urge one forward to buy, it is believed, you might skip the whole thing. What a shame!" ~ Selma Greenberg

Professional women are almost always coached to speak louder and use a more assertive tone. Because women complain that they are not noticed or heard, we assume that they need to be more noticeable by standing out more. We also assume that the male voice is preferable, easier to hear and more likely to be followed.

Therefore we tell women to lower the pitch in their voices, to breathe deeply and push from their stomachs. We tell them to turn up the volume and speak directly in a forceful, straightforward way. Speak in a manner that "commands" attention and authority. Get to the point and quickly. And most of all, stop ending sentences with an inflection or question – the deadly "tag ending."

Although women learn from their family, their friends, the television and the media to use a soft and gentle voice, particularly around men, once they enter the leadership track they are told that this type of voice is completely inappropriate. As author Susan Solovic explains, "Intimate language is fine when you're talking to your friends or your family, but in business, dynamic words demonstrate your expertise, project confidence, and demand respect."

Speaking softly and in a low voice, however, appeals to greater numbers of people and can be equally impactful. In fact by speaking slowly and calmly, others feel much more inclined to listen and better able to participate and engage. Masterful communicators know when to use each style. They know when to be direct and use an authoritative voice and when to be diffuse and use a collaborative voice.

Obviously some situations call for a more direct approach, while others require a bit of navigation. This is both a skill and a fine art. A mother of a newborn baby would use a gentle tone when nursing her child and a firmer tone when acting as principal at a school.

In my opinion most workplaces are too tolerant of sarcastic, cynical and subtly demeaning communication. The best example is the boss who combines a loud voice, an aggressive tone and threatening body language. This "bull in a china shop" wreaks havoc, yet because of his position of authority, we tolerate it.

In effect we have all come to think that a command and control voice is most effective. As non-violent communication expert Marshall Rosenberg said, we have learned this terrible way of speaking to each other over the last 8,000 years and it's time to unlearn it.

The ability to say what needs to be said in a firm yet kind manner is one of the most important skills you can learn as a social being. It is critical to both resolving conflict resolution and also relationship-building skills.

As for the "tag ending" often attributed to women, many of us assume that women are being passive when they end their sentences as if they are questions. In reality, however, women often use tag endings to be inclusive or to invite comment. Indeed they often use it intentionally. For example, when a woman ends a sentence with a question like, "It's a fine day, don't you think?" it invites the listener into the conversation by providing an opening. Just because a woman speaks this way, does not preclude her from dropping her voice and saying; "Stop that at once," on other occasions. Women learn very well when and how to speak in various contexts.

The problem therefore is not really women's voices after all but rather our judgments about women's effectiveness. Women are not seen to be effective without a strong voice. Yet it is unlikely that we would judge a woman so harshly outside the workplace. At home for example women regularly discipline children, deal with pushy sales people, and manage complex family conflicts all requiring a firm and loud voice.

The question is really this: Why do we see women (but not men) as being unable to gain compliance or demonstrate authority in the workplace because they do not use a forceful voice? Why is an aggressive tone so important at work but not in other contexts? Let me answer that question. Because we have created workplaces where this kind of male voice is seen to be effective when in other contexts it is not. Most women (and men) know that speaking forcefully is neither appropriate nor effective, so to suggest otherwise is frankly arrogant.

> **The Bottom Line.** We continually ask women to speak louder and in a more assertive tone. We have come to believe that unless women speak in a male voice, they cannot possibly be effective at leading, gaining compliance or demonstrating authority. In effect we think that a command and control style is most effective in the workplace and in business. Yet this is not true. We know that the ideal pitch, tone and vocabulary are those appropriate for each unique situation. To suggest that male voices or aggressive tones are better is too limiting for diverse workplaces and too taxing for women.

What To Do. We must stop telling women to be louder. We must challenge our societal belief that a male voice is preferable to a female voice and why a direct-command approach is preferred. We must notice the various ways in which authority and influence play out, often in a subtle manner. We need to embrace both male and female voices, tones and styles of communication and understand that all are useful and effective and can be tempered for different purposes in different contexts.

Part Three

Policies Do Make a Difference

Chapter 11

Pay and Promote Women Fairly

> "According to statistics, women make about seventy-four to seventy-six cents for every dollar earned by men. As you go up the corporate ladder, the disparity in pay widens. Executive women earn 68 percent of what their male counterparts earn.... Considering the current state of affairs, it is no surprise that many bright, talented women are fleeing corporate America to become entrepreneurs." ~ Susan Solovic

I know it might not be shocking news but here it is. In all of history, women have *never* earned as much as men in paid work. They have never earned the same pay for identical work, nor have they earned the same amount of pay for work of similar difficulty.

Recently a New Zealand equality advocacy group created a powerful advertisement for a television campaign. The very short clip shows a man driving into a parking lot and being asked by the attendant to pay 10% more for parking. When the surprised driver asks why, he is told that it is because he is a man. The message reads, "If this seems unfair to you, why do we keep paying women 10% less for the same jobs held by men?" Good question.

According to the Institute for Women's Policy Research (www.iwpr.org):

> Women are almost half of the workforce. They are the equal, if not main, breadwinner in four out of ten families. They receive more college and graduate degrees than men. Yet, on average, women continue to earn considerably less than men. In 2014, female full-time workers made only 79 cents for every dollar earned by men, a gender wage gap

of 21 percent. Women, on average, earn less than men in virtually every single occupation for which there is sufficient earnings data for both men and women to calculate an earnings ratio.

Those women who leave work for a while and return to their jobs often suffer pay cuts on their return. A *Harvard Business Review* article titled "Off Ramps and On Ramps" describes research showing that although 93% of professional women who stopped working wanted to get back in. If they took more than 2 years off they faced a 40% cut in pay on their return. If they were lucky enough to find a part-time job to stay current they earned 21% less per hour than their full-time peers.

You may ask how it is that half the population is able to earn so much more than the other half. Is the work that men are doing worth so much more than the work that women are doing? Why are so many of the high-earning jobs occupied by men? What are women doing that keeps them out of highly paid jobs?

There are several reasons why women have always been and continue to be paid less than men. Historically it was seen as inappropriate for women to earn money. First, it was not only considered dirty but was seen as an insult to her father or her husband, whose honor was called into question when he did not provide for her.

Second, the historical bargain between husband and wife was that the man would earn money and provide for the family. In exchange the woman would clean the house and raise the kids. This meant that a woman would never need money because she was, in effect, receiving wages indirectly through her husband. This bargain no longer makes sense since the divorce rates are lingering at almost 50% and the reality of single mothers means women need money just as much as men and perhaps even more.

Third, because much of women's work was historically inside the home and "domestic" it was not considered as important as men's work that was more visible since it was outside the home. Women's work was also considered menial and not requiring any particular skill. To this day, the lowest-paying jobs are those similar to women's historic domestic duties, such as cleaners, nannies and seamstresses.

Although many women worked during the Second World War in factories, as men came back into the workforce women were again refused work, effectively promoting the rise of the women's liberation movement. Yet even though almost half the working population is female, and about 70% of mothers work in paying jobs, we continue to hold onto outdated beliefs about what they deserve to be paid.

To combat this pay-equity problem, in the early 1990s many governments introduced pay-equity laws requiring that women receive the same pay for work of equal value. This helped somewhat, particularly in enlightening some people to the reality of pay discrimination, but low wages can still be found everywhere, particularly in the so-called "pink ghettos" where the profession is mostly women, like factory workers and immigrant nannies.

Not only do we pay women less, we continue to pay women who work in the home nothing. In fact we do not keep a record of women's non-paid domestic or child care work. It's not even part of our GDP (Gross Domestic Product) (note the irony in using the word domestic?) and just a few years ago the Canadian government shortened the census forms and removed those questions that collected data on women's work in the home. As a result, we often have no data about these women and their contributions at all.

And to add insult to injury, women are blamed for their low wages, for "choosing" low-paying jobs (because they are often part time) and for not negotiating hard enough. Research shows that women who short-sell themselves when they fail to negotiate for higher raises (even though this behavior is due to logical risk aversion) has a long-term impact on finances.

Susan Solovic beautifully describes the dramatic compounded effects of low pay on women.

> Even though women earn less than men, their cost of living expenses remains the same. Housing, cars, insurance, clothing and food are not discounted proportionately. That means that women have less discretionary income to save and invest, which cripples their future financial security. Because women earn less and concomitantly pay in less, they will receive lower social security benefits when they retire. Additionally, the value of the employer-sponsored retirement plan will be less. Ironically, while women's retirement benefits will be far less than men's in all likelihood, they will live longer.

As for promoting women more fairly, Professor Joan C Williams and Rachel Dempsey provide a rich and extensive collection of research that says this: women receive fewer opportunities than men, and when they are given the same opportunities, are held to a higher standard. Here are some of the things they uncovered in their research.

- Men are judged on their potential while women are judged on their achievements.

- Those hiring will often adjust criteria to suit male candidates. This is called "casuistry" or the habit of misapplying general rules to rationalize behavior. In effect the job criteria are modified so as to favor a male applicant.

- Men's successes are usually attributed to skill while women's successes are often overlooked or attributed to luck.

- Women's mistakes are often remembered more often than men's and women's successes are quickly forgotten.

- Men's mistakes are often attributed to external causes, but not so for women.

- Objective requirements are applied strictly to women but leniently to men. This is called "out-group bias" that tends to favor the group you are in by "in-group favoritism." This is also called "leniency bias."

In essence bias works this way. We harbor millions of unconscious beliefs about men and women. As we are going about our lives we have a tendency to accept those actions that are consistent with these beliefs. So if we think men are more likely to be successful, we will not just look for this, but will actually help this along. If we assume that women are not likely to be successful we not only expect it, but will inadvertently help it happen. We do this to others as well as to ourselves! This gives us comfort since our pre-conceived notions are affirmed and reinforced at the same time.

Williams and Dempsey provide a perfect example of bias. "Sometimes when women are on the phone at work, it's for a personal call. Sometimes it's for a business call. The same is true for men. But bias leads people to interpret the same action differently for men and women, creating the illusion that men are more serious workers than women are and, once again, reinforcing the very stereotypes that drive the bias in the first place."

> **The Bottom Line.** Research shows that women make less money than men and are promoted less than men. They earn less than men in identical jobs, they earn less than men in jobs requiring similar skills and they earn no income for "domestic" work. Women are often blamed for not seeking higher-paying jobs and not negotiating harder for wages. At the same time, women face bias and discrimination in hiring and promotions, often when their accomplishments are not recognized.

What To Do. We need to pay women what they deserve. Any gender-based pay gap is unacceptable. We need to look at why women's jobs tend to attract lower wages, why so many women are working part time and why these jobs pay less. We need to ensure that work of equal effort and skill is paid the same. We need to look at the jobs that men hold and question why they tend to attract higher compensation; some massively higher. We also need to question why the work that women tend to do continues to be so devalued and why we don't compensate mothers for the work they do. Most importantly we need to address our unconscious biases that cause us to prefer males. At the same time, we need to teach others how to recognize bias and deal with it.

Chapter 12

Make Flexible, Part-Time and Shared Work the Norm

"In my research on why they [women] are tending to quit, I found that, far from opting out, they are being pushed out.... What I found was that many women come to the decision to stop working as a last resort. It was a highly conflicted decision that reflected a complex decision-making process with many factors – and work was typically the precipitating factor. They asked for part-time work and couldn't get it; they asked for flextime and couldn't get it. They were stigmatized and marginalized." ~ Leslie Bennetts

I am sure that if an alien came down to earth and looked at most of our corporations and workplaces, she would say something like this: "You have got to be kidding! After centuries on earth, is this the best you can do to thrive as human beings? Are brutal work conditions necessary to thrive on earth? Do you think that you have to work 24/7 and torture yourselves to earn a reasonable living? Wow, I think I will come back in 20 years and see if you can figure it out by then!"

We each step onto the treadmill each day and believe that we have no choice. We think that we must accept the ridiculous hours and stress in order to pay our mortgages and raise our children. As a lawyer, I came to see the 24/7 workplace as the norm and a necessary "cost of doing business." I was convinced that if I did not work these ridiculous hours, somehow another law firm would steal all our clients, we would fail as a firm and I would be on the streets – destitute. Sadly, many of us believe this at some level.

We have come to think that it's acceptable to work all through the night to get a project "just right." We get called into evening meetings and no one asks whether we might have other obligations, events or perhaps family members who are depending on us at home. We see perfectionism as a badge of honor and we take pride in being called a workaholic. This behavior has become so normal that we do not even see it, let alone question its absurdity.

We shovel down fast food because it takes too long to shop for fresh, healthy food. We have no time to make nutritious meals so we consume vitamin supplements. We don't have time for a walk so we squeeze in a yoga class to maximize our fitness benefits per hour. We hire babysitters, caregivers, gardeners and meal-makers. All our friends have to be booked months ahead. Our children have anxiety issues and we wonder why.

And this accepted lifestyle and work practice is slowly killing people. It's killing nurses, lawyers, scientists and mothers. On a personal level, it is compromising our health, our families and our nurturing relationships, all silently and invisibly.

Yet we fail to see a simple fact: We have not only created this monster, but are reinforcing it simply by participating in it without question. The monster thrives by our silence and we intuitively know that if we keep feeding the beast it will devour us eventually.

Law Professor Joel Bakan, author of the book and documentary *The Corporation*, describes how the corporate model that we created makes us act in often inhumane ways. The modern corporate model is simply a machine designed for maximizing human capacity for the profits of company owners or shareholders. He explains how we invented this model to ensure economic growth and productivity but it has significant flaws that are only now becoming clear. One is the toll on the environment and the other is the toll on human beings. It clearly needs to be re-designed.

In this model, women suffer in many ways, particularly in the inflexibility of work hours. As a lawyer I was expected to bill my clients 2,400 hours a year. That's 48 hours a week. To meet this target, most lawyers have to work 80-plus hours a week since they have to "take time off" to think, eat and interact with others (called non-billable hours). It's not just the long hours, but the whole way of working at this breakneck speed that makes it not only absurd but machine-like.

And by limiting our time at home and at play, we tax our health, reduce our fitness levels, exacerbate family pressures and place enormous strain on our relationships, causing all sorts of problems.

In their book, *Getting to 50/50*, Sharon Meers and Joanna Strober review the research that shows that the 24/7 workplace is not as effective as we think. As they say, "Most bosses don't see the problem of pushing employees to the max because they get the results they want, short term, at least. The 24/7 ethic is a gross perversion of the good old-fashioned work ethic and it costs us a lot in productivity."

Leslie Perlow of Harvard's Business School conducted a 9-month study of time management practices in a Fortune 500 firm. She found that, "those who work hardest do not necessarily contribute the most to the corporation's productivity, and, in fact, that often no one benefits from this behavior, not even the corporation…if we had the incentive to get the work done in less time, we could create alternative ways of working that would be more efficient and effective."

Lying beneath these work hours and the entire corporate model are our fundamental beliefs about the way we do work. Based mostly on industrial society, we assume that people are like machines that need to be externally directed and managed. To refer to people as "human capital" is most insulting. We herd humans like cattle into tiny stalls in sterile environments. We don't think that people need to enjoy work or feel a sense of contribution. Work is a necessary evil.

These erroneous assumptions cause us to create workplaces that hold both men and women back. As the "status quo," they are rarely called into question. And although men suffer too, given women's career paths, women are impacted much more detrimentally. They tend to be the ones who give up their salaries and career paths to raise children and care for elders. They are still carrying the bulk of unpaid housework.

As Sheryl Sandberg says in *Lean In*, women were caught by surprise. "During the same years that our careers demanded maximum time investment, our biology deemed that we have children. Our partners did not share the housework and child rearing, so we found ourselves with two full-time jobs. The workplace did not evolve to give us the flexibility we needed to fulfill our responsibilities at home. We anticipated none of this. We were caught by surprise."

Many organizations have introduced flexible work hours and reduced schedules, yet many people avoid it – mostly because of the stigma. Most women believe, with good reason, that any reduction in hours or availability would jeopardize their prospects for advancement. In other words they doubt that their organizations truly support workplace flexibility.

Professor Joan C. Williams and Rachel Dempsey discovered that the stigma attached to flex policies was so great that it removed all possible benefits. Not only did this stigma prevent people from taking advantage of a flexible option, if women did take time off they faced a stigma even past the time they returned to full-time hours.

As a result it not only prevented many women from getting back into full-time work, but often forced them to take reduced hours or less pay. As they say, "Unfortunately, these policies often work on paper but not in practice. While 79 percent of companies in one national survey reported that they allow at least some of their employees to change starting and quitting times, usage rates typically are low, with somewhere between 10 and 20 percent of employees participating in either a formal or an informal agreement to vary their hours."

This research suggests that those people who take advantage of flexible hours may be retaliated against by either reduced promotions or other subtle holdbacks.

They also discovered that many professional women (especially lawyers) were encouraged to take roles that involved less responsibility and limited career mobility so that they could better manage family pressures. The only problem with this so-called "mommy track" is that it was often a dead end and these women never circled back into the partnership track. This advice to take a lesser job is often called "benevolent bias" or "romantic paternalism" since it is often provided with positive intentions but still has serious negative effects on women's careers.

Susan Solovic explains:

> About ten years ago, driven by the sheer number of women in the workforce, businesses recognized the need to begin to examine work/family issues. Male executives cleverly crafted the 'mommy track,' ostensibly to accommodate working mothers. In reality, the mommy track was a sidetrack that derailed women's careers. Even more troubling was the fact that the impact of career and family was seen as a women's issue, involving nothing more than child care.

In effect women who take advantage of flexible work policies will not only have a hard time securing full-time work after a hiatus but will likely have to accept a lesser job and lower pay. Because of ageism and sexism a 40-year-old woman (particularly a mother) is considered a liability whereas a similar male is considered a young leader.

There may be a deeper reason why we refuse to adopt flextime, part-time or shared work options. As Professor Deborah Rhode says,

"The resistance to flexible or reduced schedules stems from multiple causes. Part of the problem involves the long-standing devaluation of 'women's work' in the home and many decision makers' failure to appreciate the conflicts it presents in workplaces designed by men and for men."

The Bottom Line. We each step onto the treadmill each day and believe that we have no choice. We think that we must accept the ridiculous hours and high stress. We fail to see a simple fact: We have not only created this monster – this corporate model – we are reinforcing it simply by participating in it without question. Women are particularly impacted due to their commitments outside of work, particularly family obligations. Those who do take time off or work part time or flextime are often penalized. They find it hard to get back in, are required to accept lesser positions and pay and suffer a stigma that sticks for a very long time.

What To Do. We need to rethink our absurd fast-paced, industrial-based corporate model. This starts by believing that we can have *both* a good job and a sane life at the same time. We must admit that 24/7 means "sweatshop." Indeed many businesses have shown that it is possible to thrive without requiring that employees become slaves. As for women, we need to think of flextime, shared work and taking leaves from work as the norm. This will reduce the stigma and help to ensure that women don't suffer penalties for taking advantage of a flexible option should they wish to better balance work and family obligations.

Chapter 13

Don't Blame Women for Self-Sabotage

> "Why do [women] leave home to take their services and talents into the marketplace? Money? For sure. But maybe the need to materialize. You had to have been there to know what it was like to be invisible. To move and not be seen, to talk and not be heard. To have family return to the house every evening and say, 'Anyone home?'" ~ Erma Bombeck

Not long ago I participated in a workshop for women on how to become better negotiators. It was based partially on the research and book by Linda Babcock and Sara Laschever called *Ask for It*. The facilitator recounted several studies that showed in no uncertain terms that women were not only poor negotiators compared to men, but were actually "self-sabotaging" negotiations. According to the research, women:

- Did not recognize when they could negotiate;
- Were generally afraid of negotiation;
- Did not feel as though negotiation was authentic;
- Felt they were treated differently than men; and
- Did not think they had much power.

As a result, women tended to ask for less and received less than men did in a similar situation. Many people look at this research and think that women are simply not trying hard enough. They think that women are either incompetent or not smart enough to know what it takes to negotiate properly.

This is not the whole picture. Indeed, in order to see what is really going on for women we need to look back on their upbringing. What on the surface may look like lack of confidence is actually something very different and becomes apparent when we look at the socialization of girls and boys. It explains not only why women behave in this way, but also why we criticize women and blame them for being unskilled or naive. It also explains why we see these behaviors as self-sabotage as opposed to self-protecting, which they are.

From the moment girls are born, they are treated differently than boys. Girls are held closer and talked to in softer, more soothing tones. Girls are rescued more and boys are encouraged to be active. Media messages tell our girls to be "pretty like mommy" and our boys to be "smart like daddy." And it does not stop there. Girls are told to be nice, kind and compliant. Indeed, silence and obedience are replaced with intelligence as the commodity or power source of teen girls.

As described in the book *Lean In*:

> From a very early age, boys are encouraged to take charge and offer their opinions. Teachers interact more with boys, call on them more frequently, and ask them more questions. Boys are also more likely to call out answers, and when they do, teachers usually listen to them. When girls call out, teachers often scold them for breaking the rules and remind them to raise their hands if they want to speak.

Through all this slow socialization, girls develop a conception about who they are and who they are not through observation, imitation and identification with people and the media. We learn from others, we model them and we act in accordance with their opinions and standards.

This socialization starts in childhood and is reinforced throughout our entire lives. As a result, it becomes a self-fulfilling prophecy. Because we see men in the top leadership positions, we assume that women can't get those jobs so we don't even try. This happens as well with pay and promotions. Men generally get paid more and get promoted more often, so we expect women to earn less and get promoted less. And they do.

This explains to a large degree why women only apply for jobs if they think they meet all of the job criteria, whereas men will apply if they think they meet 60%. This socialization also explains why women so often feel like frauds, consistently underestimating ourselves because we can't believe we have made it this far. In a similar vein many studies show women tend to judge their own performance as worse than it actually is, while men judge their performance as better than it actually is.

Perhaps the most harmful socialization involves the pressure to be nice. Often called the "tyranny of niceness," girls and women are required to be nice to absolutely everyone. As described by Babcock and Laschever: "Despite all the gains we've made, one double standard (at least) persists: In our society we expect women to be nice. And it's not just that we like nice women. We think women *should* be nice – warm, pleasant, friendly. When women behave in ways that we don't perceive as warm, pleasant, and friendly...we react negatively."

As Babcock and Laschever say, there is no such expectation for men:

> Research shows that men can be influential and effective even if people don't like them. They can be persuasive and get what they want as long as they're perceived as competent. If they behave in aggressive ways or use aggressive language we call them no-nonsense, focused, a go-getter, and ambitious (good things in a man). We use very different words to describe women who behave in similar ways. Words that aren't so nice: bossy, pushy, overbearing, haughty, difficult, dragon lady, barracuda, bitch, or ice queen.

This indicates two things. Men are at an advantage because other men do not react badly to men asking for what they want, even in an aggressive way. Men can push hard to promote their own interests and are less likely to be punished for being aggressive. It also shows the huge risk to women. Women risk developing a reputation for being difficult and not a team player and being excluded from social and professional networks. This leaves women at a severe disadvantage and terribly vulnerable when they are left out of the loop in making important decisions and when they are not given good work or referred by colleagues. This is the kiss of death.

The best article I have ever read on female self-sabotage relates to the way women communicate. Women are often told that they speak too softly, don't brag enough and often put themselves down too often. Although usually this is seen as problematic behavior, academic Dayle Smith looked at this in a completely different light in *Women at Work*.

Smith found that the main communication patterns that women use, that often get judged negatively, are actually designed to accomplish a specific purpose, both consciously and unconsciously. For example, women tend to speak in a quiet voice, because they do not want to appear pushy and want to encourage others' comments. They tend to ask questions, not because they have no answer, but rather because they would prefer to hear from others first. Rather than seeing women as self-sabotaging, the researchers saw them as highly adaptive and masterful, skills often used for survival.

Most fantastic is the fact that the primary motivation behind most of women's communication is the desire to build relationships. This is supported by the research of Professor Deborah Tannen, who found that a primary goal for women in conversation was to create connection while a primary goal for men was to demonstrate personal competence or strength. This explains why men's actions often appear competitive and women's actions often look congenial. Women often think men are arguing and men think women are being passive.

In addition to simply holding women back, this intensive socialization of women has been shown to cause depression and mental illness (no surprise here). Have you ever wondered why so many women are taking medications for stress and anxiety? Research suggests that it may be a gender issue. In their book, *The Cost of Competence*, Brett Silverstein and Deborah Perlick state, "If we belong in categories that are negatively evaluated, our own sense of identity and self-worth is likely to suffer." Indeed women start losing self-esteem in their teen years when girls realize that they will be forever limited by society because they are female. As they say, "From the time they were young girls, these women confronted a model of adult femininity associated with limitations, low status, unhappiness, and lack of respect. At adolescence these girls were 'thrown'...into the role of woman that they had seen so devalued."

> **The Bottom Line.** We often accuse women of self-sabotaging and being their own worst enemies. We point to their hesitation to speak up and negotiate for what they deserve. By stepping back and looking at the socialization of females we see that women are simply products of intense and ongoing socialization that teaches them to be nice, kind, quiet and compliant. In this light we see that women are not self-sabotaging, they are just being nice, putting others first and building connections, as they have been taught. When they are told to be tough, they feel conflicted and often suffer in other ways. As Sheryl Sandberg says, "No wonder women don't negotiate as much as men. It's like trying to cross a minefield backward in high heels."

What To Do. When women do not negotiate aggressively or speak out, we can no longer blame them for self-sabotage. We must instead look at the intense socialization (from childhood and ongoing) to be nice, complaint and helpful. This often causes women to sacrifice they own ambitions and success. We must notice this tendency and stop taking advantage of it. We must educate people about what is really going on, start accepting females for who they are and begin to appreciate their feminine strengths.

Chapter 14

Deal with Discrimination and Sexism

"For most of recorded history, women were largely excluded from formal leadership positions. A comprehensive review of encyclopedia entries published just after the turn of the last century identified only about 850 eminent women, famous or infamous, throughout the preceding two thousand years.... Few of these women had acquired leadership positions in their own right. Most exercised influence through relationships with men."
~ Deborah Rhode

Whether we want to admit it or not, we all discriminate against females. We treat women and girls in very different ways than men and boys just because they are female. This is called sexism or bias on the basis of gender. It is extremely common and very harmful.

Over three thousand years we have inherited both outdated notions about females and habitual behaviors that cause each and every one of us to hold women back. We treat women worse because they are female, we limit their choices and we extend fewer freedoms and opportunities to women than men.

We like to think that it does not exist, but it does. Common discriminatory or sexist practices include hiring more men than women, not hiring mothers, firing women when they get pregnant and not hiring mothers after maternity leaves. Although human rights laws were introduced to combat this type of sexism, making it illegal and levying fines against corporations, laws do not eradicate sexism. In fact most of it has gone underground and today's sexism is often subtle and takes place behind closed doors.

Here are some typical discriminatory ideas that people tend to have about professional women.

- Don't hire a woman because she will likely get pregnant and quit.

- Don't hire a woman because she won't fit in this culture.

- Don't give that work to a woman because she is not tough enough.

- Don't promote a woman because a man competing for her job needs the job more.

- Don't give an office to a woman because she does not need it as much as a man.

- Don't give difficult or high-profile work to a woman because it is not suitable.

- Don't give women financial work because they aren't very good at numbers.

These thoughts may sound old-fashioned but I assure you they are not. Indeed, the most damaging are those of which we are unaware. In many instances, our programming is so deep we don't even realize we are discriminating.

One of the most obvious types of bias that shows up every day in workplaces is role stereotyping. Without even realizing it, we harbor bundles of ideas about what type of work men and women can and should do. For example, we still think that men should be doctors and women should be nurses. In general terms we think that men are (or should be) providers, breadwinners and leaders so we offer them high paying jobs as the heads of corporations. We think that women are (or should be) homemakers and caregivers so we offer them support roles such as administration or secretarial work.

But worse than that, when women step out of their narrowly defined stereotypical roles, they are often condemned as odd, inappropriate or too masculine. And even more insidious is this: when a woman does very well in a male-type job or career, we assume this is either very strange or not possible. So we make up stories about her, such as: she is a man in women's clothing or she is a robot and has no personal life.

Over time many women come to believe that these stereotypes are true and internalize them. Deborah Rhode found that many women come to believe that they are both incompetent at leadership and not deserving enough to lead. As a result they do not expect rewards for performance and they lack confidence to take risks. Like a self-fulfilling prophecy, as described above, it explains to a large degree why women are blamed for self-sabotage. Although women do not intentionally cut themselves short, they have simply come to believe they cannot get what they want. Like the psychological concept of learned helplessness, those who are repeatedly shut down eventually give up even trying.

Rhode suggests that this also explains why others are less likely to view women as leaders. For example when a man is seated at the head of the table for a meeting, we assume he is the leader. We do not make the same assumptions about women, nor do we accord them the same deference.

Another way we discriminate is by valuing men's work and masculine characteristics more than women's work and feminine characteristics. For example, research shows that characteristics traditionally associated with leadership are masculine traits such as assertiveness and directness. Yet when women take on these masculine characteristics, they are frowned upon. Rhode found that in an examination of more than a hundred studies involving the evaluation of leaders, women are ranked lower when they adopt a "masculine" authoritative style, particularly when the evaluators are men. "Women who take strong positions risk being stereotyped as 'bitchy,' 'difficult,' or 'manly.' Women who try to avoid those assessments risk losing ground to men who are more assertive."

Professor Joan C. Williams and Rachel Dempsey describe another particular type of bias that hits women when they decide to become mothers. This so-called "maternal wall" consists of the following:

- Labeling women who get pregnant as mother rather than career women – leading to a questioning of a woman's competence and commitment.

- Remembering the specific instances when mothers deal with family matters (like attend emergencies), even years after the event.

- Seeing women's absences for family matters as a pattern as opposed to a fluke, as they do with men's absences.

- Assuming that absences from the office by women are for family matters as opposed to business matters.

- Expecting that pregnant women and mothers will act in a more caring and nurturing manner than men or non-mothers.

- Assuming the birth of a child for a man will mean increased commitment but for a woman decreased commitment.

As they say, "Good workers put their jobs first; good mothers put their children first" and "Employers discriminate against mothers because they believe mothers 'should' be at home with their children. Mothers who demonstrate high levels of commitment to paid work violate prescriptive stereotypes about the appropriate place for women."

One lawyer who was interviewed describes it this way: "If you're being a good lawyer you're not a good mother, and if you are being a good mother, you can't be a good lawyer. If you are staying all night at work, there's no way you can be a good mother. And if you are asking to go home early or try to get permission to work from home, there's no way you can be a good professional."

According to Susan Solovic in *The Girls' Guide to Power and Success*:

> Thanks to federal and state legislation that makes sexual harassment and sexual discrimination illegal, the incidents of blatant and egregious conduct, such as the boss chasing his secretary around the desk, are rare although not completely non-existent. However, the statutory protection has not been successful in precluding more subtle forms of discrimination. There are a myriad of clever ways to block women from the top without being obvious. For example, a company can give a woman the title of vice president, but limit the scope of her authority.... There are unwritten rules that all the men at the top seem to know and adhere to. Although these men know the politically correct things to say, with a wink and a nod they do something else.

In the 1960s and 70s women became more educated and more active in battling sexism and pushed to have laws introduced to stop discrimination. Today we have laws that make it illegal for employers to discriminate against a woman when hiring and promoting just because she is a woman. Other laws require that women receive equal pay for equal work and for work of equal value. Still, this does not stop discrimination and often just pushes it underground.

Many organizations have tried to stop sexism through affirmative action. This means taking active steps to push women up the ladder. Usually it includes introducing quotas for women, such as requiring that equal numbers of men and women are interviewed for a position. Often the first step is simply keeping track of the numbers of hires, promotions, demotions and departures of women relative to men.

Although some people think this is a sledgehammer approach and flies in the face of merit-based hiring and promoting, it does force us to recognize some of the blinders that prevent us from seeing females as assets to organizations. Recently a securities commission created a law requiring that all publicly traded corporations collect and make public information about the number of women on their boards. This alone has caused many companies (particularly in the resource sector) to scramble to find women board members.

Many organizations spend hundreds of hours and millions of dollars each year fighting in the courts to have discriminatory laws and practices overturned. I worked with one, Women's Legal Education and Action Fund (LEAF), which helped fight several famous legal cases. It was costly, difficult and time consuming work simply to get women's rights for equality recognized.

> **The Bottom Line.** We all harbor biases about women. We assume they are sensitive and nurturing. We assume they do not want or could not handle complex tasks. Because of this we treat women unfairly on the basis of their sex. This sexism or discrimination is everywhere. We pay and promote women less and we slot them into stereotypical roles, particularly mothers. Although sexism is obviously unfair and in many cases illegal, much of it exists because of unconscious beliefs. For example, we think that women do not really belong in leadership roles and are not as competent or committed as males. Sadly, many people do not recognize this, nor do they think there is anything wrong with it. Yet sexism is one of the main ways in which women are held back.

What To Do. We are not born sexist. Each of us inherits outdated ideas about women (and men) and they need to be updated to reflect our current reality. Now. This will be hard work since most sexism is caused by subconscious beliefs that we often don't even know exist. We must stop stereotyping women as secretaries, mothers, bitches or anything else! Women deserve to be treated better at home, at work and in society. It is illegal and fundamentally unfair to treat one human being worse than another for no other reason than because they were born female. We must teach our children early that women and men are equal – no better or worse, no stronger or weaker. Sexism must stop.

Chapter 15

Stop Sexual Harassment

> "That our daughters must endure pinching, grabbing, persistent requests for dates, and suggestive comments in a place where they are required by law to be, seems degrading if not criminal." ~ Jeanne Elium and Don Elium

One particularly bothersome type of discrimination is sexual harassment. Sexual harassment means harassing another on the basis of sex. It means offending or bothering females just because they are female. This includes sexist jokes, unwanted staring, whistles, brushing up against women, mean rumors, cruel writing on walls and comments in an e-mail.

In 2014, a short video on sexual harassment went viral, getting more than a million views in a few hours. The video was posted on YouTube by Hollaback!, an international movement devoted to ending street harassment and produced by a group called the Everyday Sexism Project and a professional videographer. In it, a woman is shown simply walking down the streets of New York City for one whole day.

Dressed casually in black pants, black shirt and low shoes, she walked for 10 full hours up and down the streets not saying a word and not interacting with anyone. It was all filmed by a hidden camera. When the producers reviewed the tape and counted the number of times men made propositions to her, they were shocked to discover that she had been approached 106 times! And worse than that, several men followed her and said things like, "What's wrong with you?" and "Don't you think I'm good enough for you?"

How many times do you think this might happen to a man in New York City?

Almost every woman I know has been sexually harassed – although they might not recognize it at first. From sexist jokes at a dinner party that make most women cringe, to being fondled in a crowded bus, sexual harassment goes on day in and day out. In California, according to recent research, 54% of Berkeley High School's female students reported being sexually harassed while at school.

Although some think sexual harassment has gone away, nothing is further from the truth. Indeed it is often downplayed, normalized or joked about, often suggesting that it happens to everyone – males and females alike. This distorts the facts. Almost every girl and woman will experience sexual touching, degrading treatment and harassing comments many times over her lifetime in some form or other.

Worse yet, women are told to view it as a form of flattery or flirtation. I can't tell you how many times I have been told that I clearly have no sense of humor or "I would love it if you would harass me!" Every woman knows exactly how it feels to be degraded and ashamed by one random comment or subtle touch.

Sadly it seems that boys learn that harassing girls is okay. From a very young age boys tend to see girls as less valuable and less worthy of respect. They learn how to demean other boys by calling them a girl, pussy, faggot or femme. They watch abuse and pornography on the Internet and in films and learn that female means weak, pathetic and powerless. No wonder they have no idea that their harassment is problematic.

There are apparently two motivations for men who sexually harass women. One is more sexual and usually targeted at young, unmarried women in less powerful positions. In this case the man is trying to attract women and engage in sex. The other is aimed at women who are perceived as a threat to men, and the motive is to drive them away. These women are typically in male-based occupations or in managerial positions. The aim is to make the woman feel so uncomfortable that she will quit.

Either way, the often hidden truth is that sexism and sexual harassment are rarely about sex, they are about power. They are about one sex (male) declaring dominance over the other (female). These actions not only keep women feeling degraded and inferior but also keep them down and with a reduced sense of power. In other words, when males make inappropriate comments at women it is a way of asserting power. In effect it is saying that I am the boss of you and I am the one who decides how you can be treated, not you.

Author Anita Roberts suggests that, "The purpose of these types of remarks is not to enhance self-esteem but to assert status. When males do this they are reminding you (and themselves) that you are female and they are male and therefore of higher status. Insecure males tend to make these comments particularly when they feel threatened or challenged in some way by a female."

In my experience as a lawyer, much of workplace sexual harassment is about keeping women in their place by creating a hostile environment – intentionally or unintentionally. Every single degrading or uncomfortable comment chips away at a woman's self-worth, sense of achievement and sense of belonging. In fact that is what they were designed for. Those men who complain that it is impossible to "know what women want these days" show a serious lack of empathy since the difference between flattery and harassment is fairly obvious to those experiencing it. In simple terms, flattery makes a woman feel good and harassment makes her feel bad. A real compliment isn't confusing.

The Bottom Line. Women often experience sexual harassment. Just walking down a street can invite rude comments from men who are asserting their authority and power. From catcalls to leering and physical touching, it is as if some men feel they are permitted to behave in this publicly degrading and humiliating manner. What many men who harass do not realize is that harassment is not only insulting and degrading but eventually erodes women's sense of self-worth and confidence. It is also a larger reflection of how we view females in society and the invisible power imbalance that favors men.

What To Do. We must stop pretending that sexual harassment does not exist or is in some way okay. We must make it clear to boys and men that this type of treatment of females is not only wrong but terrorizing. We must also look more deeply at the concept of privilege and why boys and men harass in the first place. Do they think that it is okay? Are men aware of the impact that harassment has on women? Women should never be afraid to go outside or go to work fearing they will be approached uninvited.

Part Four

If We Really Want Women to Succeed

Chapter 16

Provide Access to Mentors, Networks and Women

"Participation in informal networks is particularly difficult for women with demanding family commitments, who lack time for the social activities that could generate collegial support and client contacts.... Men pick up career tips; women pick up laundry, kids, dinner, and the house. The result is that many women remain out of the loop of career development."

~ Deborah Rhode

Successful women tell me repeatedly that they have tried to break into the "boys' club." They tell stories of golfing lessons on their personal time, smoking cigars and even eating at strip bars. Some women get invited along and pretend they are just one of the guys.

Most women, however, are simply not invited. These women tend to rationalize, suggesting that men simply prefer men's company. There is nothing wrong with that. Yet by being excluded, women have significantly less opportunity for camaraderie, access to contacts and, more disturbing, advancement. Because so much business happens in the boys' clubs, they inadvertently hold women back.

You might recall the battles of the 1980s, when women fought to become members in professional men's clubs. Almost all influential business and networking clubs were men-only clubs. Ranchmen's clubs, engineers' clubs, geologists' clubs and architects' clubs did not allow women to become members. The members of these clubs argued (often fiercely in courtrooms) that women did not belong primarily because these clubs were merely social venues and did not involve business networking. Men simply wanted to socialize with men. Women had their own clubs (or not).

No one would dispute the freedom to associate, yet by keeping women out, they missed out on many referrals, new business and promotions. The cost of excluding women was so high that eventually many laws were changed, forcing certain clubs to open their doors to women. Even today, although women are welcome to join, they are often excluded in other ways.

As for mentoring, research shows that while the importance of mentors has long been recognized, the mentoring of women has not only lagged behind but may be one of the biggest barriers to women moving into positions of leadership and influence. Law Professor Deborah Rhode describes the impact this way: "For many women, support of an influential senior colleague is critical in securing leadership opportunities. Mentors can sponsor women for challenging assignments and prestigious positions, as well as refer clients and provide business development opportunities."

Yet mentors are rare and picky. Powerful women who could act as mentors also have three things going against them. First, being so few, they can hardly spread themselves over all the emerging women leaders. Second, they are often not as influential or as powerful as they appear. Many still feel vulnerable, sensing that they may just be a token and easily removed or replaced. Some women hesitate helping other women under the perception that another "weak" woman might weigh them down. Third, women in positions of power are not always ideal mentors unless they are willing to challenge the status quo. Some senior women think younger women should "suck it up" by accepting it and move on.

Riane Eisler explains why senior women act this way in hierarchical organizations. In her book, *The Power of Partnership,* she says, "The problem, however, is that if women find themselves in dominator organizations, they attain positions of authority only if they take on stereotypically masculine or 'hard' ways of operating. You see this in the famous case of the tough policies and management style of former British Prime Minister Margaret Thatcher, sometimes referred to as 'the best man in England.'"

In other words, many women at the top see the ladder as a necessary evil, rarely questioning the current corporate ladder and often encouraging others to accept it and get on with things. They urge women to stop whining and learn how to "play the game."

In their book, Professor Joan C. Williams and Rachel Dempsey dedicate an entire section to the difficulties women face in relation to other women. Calling it a "tug of war" they suggest that these struggles are not only a major barrier to women's success, but one of the main results of gender bias. They found that women not only fail to support each other but often view each other as competition and resort to judging and sabotaging each other. Importantly, however, women are not entirely to blame for this behavior. Research shows that female rivalry in the workplace is a direct result of sexism at work and in society, as these findings suggest.

- Women think that they need to undercut other women if they hope to attain the only seat at the table.

- A sense of competition is bred by the idea that opportunities for women are rare.

- Women can penalize other women when they themselves are feeling vulnerable.

- A combat-like culture strains relationships between women.

- Women are expected to be nice to everyone and, if not, are often labeled bitches.

- Many women think that women are intrinsically less able and committed than men.

- Some women distance themselves from other women for fear of being stereotyped and avoid women if they think it will hold them back.

- Professional women can be hard on female assistants as they try to prove themselves and female assistants often expect kinder and gentler behavior from female bosses.

- The media reinforces stereotypes that portray successful women as selfish, evil and bad, as in the film, *The Devil Wears Prada*.

As for male mentors, they too are rare and often see little benefit to mentoring women. It does not tend to advance them or their careers. Men will sometimes mentor daughters of colleagues or family friends as a favor to another man. Given the propaganda about sexual misconduct and the real danger of a male asserting his power over a young mentee, many men are simply not willing to take the risk.

Sheryl Sandberg describes male mentoring this way:

> This means that men will often gravitate toward sponsoring younger men, with whom they connect more naturally. Since there are so many more men at the top of every industry, the proverbial old-boy network continues to flourish. And since there are already a reduced number of women in leadership roles, it is not possible for the junior women to get enough support unless the senior men jump in too.

So the question remains – like an elephant in the room – do men as a group really want to advance women so that they can be their true equals? I don't think it's a conspiracy per se, but there is a general lack of interest in helping women. Most women find that, one-on-one, men enjoy their company and want them to succeed. Yet, when in the company of other males, men rarely outwardly promote women and behind closed doors when men don't stand up for women, they often inadvertently take women down, not realizing the full impact.

It reminds me of a talk I attended. A young man was speaking about how men conducted business and why women were losing out. He told us about a disturbing reality called "the deep six" strategy that men use when they feel threatened by a woman. Apparently a conversation between two men will go something like this: "Hey Bob, do you know Cathy Berenson? I am thinking of promoting her." The other man replies something like this: "Yes, Cathy is really nice and she seems smart but I am not sure I would trust her completely." That's it. End of conversation. Nothing else is said. Meanwhile Cathy does not get the promotion but, worse yet, she has no idea what she did wrong and is powerless to fight what she cannot see.

> **The Bottom Line.** Research shows that professional women not only have fewer mentoring opportunities than men but are often excluded from networking and relationship building activities. Both are important to women's sense of camaraderie and real advancement. Often men will lunch together, golf together and club together without any women in sight. Business will get done and women will never know it happened. Senior male mentors are rare and often do not see an advantage to mentoring women. Women mentors are rarer still, given the few women in leadership positions, and also hesitate to mentor women for a complex set of reasons.

What To Do. It's important for men as a group to step up on this. Senior men in particular have to both open their networks to women and open their eyes to not just the value of women but to the possibility of seeing women as true partners. The silos we have built between men and women need to be slowly pulled down. As for mentoring, men in leadership positions need to recognize the difficulties women face at work and in finding mentors. They need to realize that much of the knowledge they possess and the support they can offer can make or break it for women.

As for women mentors, we need to look at our hierarchical culture and untangle the reasons women-to-women mentoring and women rivalry is so problematic. We need powerful women's groups to offer advice and support. As Williams and Dempsey say, "It's time for women to stop judging each other about what they believe to be the right way to be a woman. In workplaces still dominated by men, all women make compromises. If we begin to judge each other's compromises, the opportunity for women to help each other vanishes."

Chapter 17

Provide Support for Life and Family

> "They face compromises that men do not share. Their right to 'choose' – to remain true to themselves, to make (and act upon) their own choices – is systematically curtailed when they become mothers. And that's because the structures of our society as they currently exist do not allow mothers to make meaningful choices. Too many are forced to abdicate the dreams of a lifetime because the demands of the workplace are incompatible with family life. Others, in the quest to support their families, must 'choose' to consign their children to seriously substandard care. Others must abdicate their dreams of homemaking because it is simply too costly...." ~ Judith Warner

In 2012 Anne-Marie Slaughter, a former Director of Policy and Planning at the US State Department wrote an article and later presented a TED talk that opened up the proverbial can of worms by asking: How on earth do women who want high-powered jobs also raise children?

Her article, titled "Why Women Still Can't Have it All" (*Atlantic Magazine*), was read by millions and re-ignited the dormant conversation about why we make workplaces so impossible for women. This article identified the very real things that pushed women off the fast track and dispelled the idea that women leave for their children. It blames bias and discrimination instead.

Years ago I met a lawyer who did not believe in discrimination or sexism. Like many other women, she had stopped practicing law when her two children entered school. She introduced herself as a stay-at-home mom, not a former high-powered lawyer. When I told her that I was writing a book on the glass ceiling, she became very agitated. I obviously hit a nerve when I suggested women were being held back by having to choose between career and family.

She told me quite forcefully that she "chose" to quit law and felt no pressure at all to do so. It was her free choice. She had spent significant time considering her options and speaking with her husband. Ultimately she decided that the best thing for her was to quit paid work and stay at home full time with her children. She said she felt lucky to be able to manage on only her husband's income. As she said, she simply did not want to work herself to the bone to be both a lawyer and a stressed-out mom.

When I suggested that it must have been a difficult choice, she disagreed. She made her choice freely and had weighed all the benefits and costs. Although she felt she could both practice law and raise her children, she was not willing to make "those kinds of sacrifices." She told me that I was dreaming to believe that things could change

This is a typical example of a woman who has fallen for the "rhetoric of choice." In simple terms, rhetoric is a sequence of logical propositions that leads to a single narrow answer or outcome. It hides the truth in words buried in a stream of assumptions and mistruths. Advertisers are masters at this art, as are governments that like to use propaganda to convince people of something. The only way to combat rhetoric is by asking many questions, teasing apart the logic and opening up the truth.

The "choice" we give mothers in our society today may appear *free* but it is extraordinarily narrowed by the options. In effect we place women between a rock and a hard place. Those women who want a family life and also a career are given this narrow choice: If they choose to have a family, they must sacrifice their family or their job. They cannot have both (like men can). If they want to have high-paying and demanding careers as executives or CEOs, they must hire someone else to care for their children because the work is not flexible. If they really want to raise a family, they cannot take on a job of any significant responsibility, influence or authority because it's mutually exclusive.

Sheryl Sandberg describes it as follows:

> Women are surrounded by headlines and stories warning them that they cannot be committed to both their families and careers. They are told over and over again that they have to choose, because if they try to do too much, they'll be harried and unhappy. Framing the issue as "work-life balance" – as if the two were diametrically opposed – practically ensures work will lose out. Who would ever choose work over life?

In her book *Perfect Madness*, Judith Warner found that, "The demands of the contemporary workplace, which often require long working hours and long commutes, force mothers to separate from their children for excessive periods of time. Lack of flexibility completes a picture in which women really *are* forced to choose between providing for and nurturing their children."

As Warner says, the so-called "choices" most of us face – between full-time work or 24/7 on-duty motherhood – are, "quite simply, *unnatural*. They amount to a kind of psychological castration: excessive work severs a mother from her need to be physically present in caring for her child, and excessive 'full-time' motherhood of the total-reality variety severs a mother, not only from her ability to financially provide for her family but also from her adult *sense of agency* as it sucks her so deeply down into the infantile realm of her children."

What we fail to see underlying this impossible choice is that other factors are at play. Not only do we have inflexible workplaces but we also lack family supports that might make balancing much easier.

One missing support that is often the death knell to women's careers is child support. Starting from the birth of a child to the day that child leaves home, parents carry the full weight of feeding, clothing and raising their children. In practical terms this means that a parent either stays home and cares for the children (often sacrificing a career) or they pay someone to care for them. Unless employers provide maternity leaves and other time off to care for children, parents have no choice but to quit or to pay someone else to raise their children – even if the cost is more than their take-home pay.

Many governments worldwide lift some of this burden off parents by making laws so that parents can take maternity leaves and access other child supports and programs. This is not just so mothers can continue to work (and pay taxes) but also because without these supports many families slip into poverty and children go hungry and flounder.

But the United States is not one of these countries. As Joan C. Williams and Rachel Dempsey point out, although about 95% of all developed countries have 14 weeks or more of maternity leave, the United States is the only developed country to have no nationally mandated maternity leave. As they say,

> The United States also lacks many other provisions that help reconcile work and family in other countries. These include worker protections such has mandatory vacations, part-time parity (proportional pay and advancement for part-time work), limits of mandatory overtime, and the right to request a flexible schedule. The United States also lacks high-quality subsidized child care, after-school programs and adult day care. It even lacks paid sick days. As a result, Americans report higher levels of work-family conflict than do the citizens of other industrialized countries.

As suggested by Warner, child care is a political, systemic issue. If mothers cannot access quality child care, they cannot do other meaningful work, paid or unpaid. They will feel they have no choice.

Have you ever wondered why school hours are typically 9 to 3 and work hours are typically 9 to 5? How about dentists' and doctors' hours? How about teachers' professional development days? And the days when kids are sick? It's frankly impossible for a parent who works 9 to 5 (with a few weeks of vacation and a few statutory holidays) to also take the time needed to care for kids, to take them to appointments and to provide care when schools are closed. The time needed to care for the average child adds up to about 45 days each year!

And men are not helping much. Research by Deborah Rhode shows that, "despite a significant increase in men's domestic work over the last two decades, women continue to shoulder the major burden." And to compound matters, "the demands of bearing and caring for young children are most intense during the same period in which the foundations for career development are laid."

As Williams and Dempsey say:

> In a country where the workplace is structured around an ideal worker who's on call 24/7 and motherhood is characterized by the model of a mother always available to her children, it's hard to balance work and family. No news there. What's more controversial is to call this phenomenon gender bias but when 82 percent of American women — and 76 percent of women with an advanced degree — have children at home at some point in their lives, how can we call it anything else?

The Bottom Line. One of the biggest hurdles holding a woman back is her children. As soon as a child is born, it is typically mothers who carry the burden of raising children, often having to sacrifice careers in the process. Although we call this a "free choice" the truth is that we have created a work world in which it's almost impossible for women to have both a career and a family. We make the work hours and responsibilities (at both work and home!) so onerous that work-life balance is impossible. We don't provide flexible hours or supports so that mothers can still work while caring for children and we allow husbands and fathers to participate in family at a very minimal level, leaving women overwhelmed.

What To Do. First we must understand that women, just like men, want and often need to work for pay. Many want a meaningful and high-paying career. No woman should feel that she has to choose between a career and a family, and to ask women to choose is like forcing her to make a "Sophie's choice" (between two children). We must start adjusting our workplaces build in flextime, part-time and shared work so that it becomes the norm – without a stigma. If we truly want to free up women to be full participants at work, then corporations and governments need to provide supports to raise the next generation. This includes maternity/paternity leaves and childcare. At the same time, we have to stop expecting men to work 24/7 and encourage them to engage equally in child-rearing and housework.

Chapter 18

Encourage Women to Seek Power

> "[The] challenge to traditional femininity has not been complete. Lurking just below the surface of society's tolerant acceptance, there exists a deep ambivalence toward female power and achievement – rewarding it one minute, ignoring it the next, even vilifying it on occasion." ~ Nicky Marone

Many people criticize women for not asserting themselves or stepping into their power. Indeed, I often get accused of trying to be too nice, being too shy, putting myself down or downplaying my accomplishments. Yet this is not the problem at all. I am not overly humble or modest. I am simply behaving in a way that is acceptable – as a woman.

I am playing out the (less powerful) role expected of me and I am also "asserting" my power in the way that I have learned throughout my life, which is through connections and relationships and not through dominance. Unfortunately, however, this behavior causes me and other women all sorts of problems.

We miss out on opportunities to share our experiences and brilliance. Other people do not know what we have to offer and thus overlook us when considering promotions and new opportunities. Indeed shrinking from our own power and hiding in an effort to belong or include others may be one of the worst ways to get noticed or promoted inside an organization or outside in the public realm – either as a woman or a man.

So how can we deal with this aversion to power and more importantly, were does it come from?

Have you ever noticed how a woman will rarely, if ever, mention power? She will never talk about her salary and will often downplay the fact that she has loads of money or is the owner of a business. Many women will intentionally divert a conversation to avoid the talk of power and status completely. Indeed most women get very uncomfortable or embarrassed when the topic of power is raised.

Yet it is the opposite with many men. Not only do men talk about power, they often brag about it. If you listen closely, the topic of success and power is the undercurrent of many male-to-male conversations. You hear things such as what company took over another; who took over the top job; who secured the most funding; etc. Men often openly boast about quarterly results, six-figure incomes and golf scores.

This is so for two reasons. Women are raised to give away their power and at the same time are socialized to put others first. In doing so we inadvertently accept a type of secondary role in our society.

From a very young age girls are actively discouraged from asserting power. In her book *Safe Teen*, Anita Roberts lists a few of the ways in which we socialize girls to give up their power. We expect girls to:

- Ask permission to speak;
- Be modest and not proud;
- Apologize;
- Allow men to fill in names, figures and dates;
- Be patient, quiet and not speak up;
- Smile even when not happy;
- Avoid confrontation by conceding; and
- Not defend their boundaries or say "no."

Girls also learn to put others first. Indeed to appear "better" than another person, particularly a boy or man, is a terrible thing. Inclusion is the name of the game and niceness and politeness are required behaviors. In other words we must never put ourselves before anyone else. Wives must bow to husbands. Mothers must serve the family first. Women must wait until everyone's needs have been met before their own. A woman who pushes her way to the front of the line would be considered contrary.

The related message (that no one dares to talk about) is that women must never appear more powerful than men. We are told that this can cause some men to feel weak, bad about themselves or "less than" another. As a result we learn to downplay our own abilities and talents and, most importantly, to never publicly embarrass a man. And of course bragging or making yourself seem "better" is the precise thing that might cause this to happen.

This was one of the most painful lessons I ever learned as a lawyer and it happened to me a few times before I realized what was going on. I learned that pointing out any mistakes or oversights of a male lawyer had to be done with kid gloves. As a result I usually refrained from giving any feedback at all since it often seemed that, even if I candy-coated my comments in diplomatic language, they were often perceived as an insult and "take down."

Most women know how to play this power game. They know that if they want to be successful they must ensure that the men around them also feel powerful. I have watched many women in social settings play what I call "the Barbara Walters interview technique." They spend their evenings simply interviewing men by asking them question after question. Many men don't mind talking about themselves and many women don't mind not talking about themselves. But in doing this, women do not take the opportunity to share or shine.

One of the best ways to observe power dynamics is by listening to male-female conversations. For example, you might notice a woman flatter a man on his intelligence or attire. These women are often unconsciously and quite naturally elevating men. As a result, men will feel better about themselves. But men only return the compliment if they are trying to even the score. Indeed men often view this type of flattery as putting themselves down, which is not a good thing if they are trying to garner respect.

Although these power dynamics are at play all the time, we do not see them and what they tell us about our role in society. Lurking below the surface is a sense that the role of women is to appease men or be helpful to men and not be better than men.

Here is an exercise I often give to audiences to help them explore the difference between male and female perspectives on power in conversation.

> Imagine two strangers, a man and a woman, walking into a bar. They begin talking about their shared interest in downhill skiing. She says, "I am planning to go to Aspen this year, have you ever been there?" He responds by saying, _____ [ask audience to fill in blank]. For example, "I have been there many times. It is amazing!"
>
> I then ask the audience to switch roles. Imagine it was the man who was planning to go to Aspen. But then I add one other fact: the woman has ski-raced her whole life and has been skiing since she was a child. In this scenario the women would respond by saying, _____ [ask audience to fill in the blank]. For example, "Oh, you are so lucky; I have a friend who lives there. Maybe she can recommend a place to stay."
>
> Then we compare the two. More often than not, men see this conversation as an opportunity to share their expertise or brag about themselves. A woman, on the other hand, will often see this as an opportunity to build a relationship and genuinely help. So then I ask the audience, "Do you think the woman told the man that she was an expert skier? Why or why not?" A great conversation always occurs.

The main reason women downplay their abilities and don't talk about power is because they think it is wrong to do so. They think it is not only inappropriate, but actually tacky and a conversation-killer. They know from experience that if they brag or look "too good" they will be shamed or rejected. A woman who brags is looking for trouble.

As a result women often unconsciously have a deep aversion to talking about power at all. The main phrase floating around in our subconscious is this: "Just who do you think you are?" In other words, how dare you think that you are somebody important or powerful?

So it comes as no surprise that, for women, the topic of power has become *the topic that shall not be mentioned*. In fact, not only is the topic taboo, but asserting or using power is also problematic for women. We repeatedly tell women that showing authority is not only non-feminine but also aggressive. A recent book titled *Am-BITCH-ous* rightly points out that throughout history women have been discouraged from showing their ambitions for fear of being rejected or being called a bitch.

And our ideas about what can befall a woman who holds too much power is reinforced every single day. Shockingly, Canada's past Prime Minister, Stephen Harper, took a low blow at one of the highest-ranking women in Canada in 2014, questioning her neutrality and ethics. Lawyers hold Madam Justice Beverley McLachlin, the Chief Justice of the Supreme Court of Canada, in the highest regard. Luckily several of the most powerful lawyers in Canada wrote strongly worded editorials to save her reputation. But still, we all saw the appalling treatment of such a brilliant, powerful and gracious woman. Another example involved the first female Australian Prime Minister, who was personally attacked repeatedly, so much that she finally had to call it for what it was: misogyny (women hating). Regardless, she lost the next election to the man who crucified her publicly.

The recent media attention around the new female CEO of Yahoo provides another example. Marissa Mayer is the poster girl for success, yet when she announced her pregnancy she became the brunt of jokes about the length of her maternity leave. If it was too short it was terrible. If it was too long it was terrible.

A few years ago two powerful female senior editors were imperceptibly fired within a week of each other. Each woman had more than 25 years of experience in the highly influential multi-billion-dollar media business. Both dismissals sent professional women around the world reeling. In the front of our minds was the following phrase: "If it can happen to them, then surely it can happen to me." Even at the pinnacle of their careers, these women seemed to be taken down simply because they had become too powerful. They overstepped that invisible line.

All of these events send a clear statement about women and power today. And the messages come equally from men and women. As author Marianne Williamson points out, "Much of the prejudice against women is stored at an unconscious level. Many of those who hold the most punishing attitudes toward passionate women – and free women are passionate women – consider themselves social liberals, even feminists. Women's rights seem to them to be of obvious importance, but what is not obvious to them is how much they conspire to keep the lid on female power."

Another taboo topic directly related to power is money. Even though money is the primary measure of power in our western society, women rarely mention it and actually avoid talking about it. Perhaps this is one of the reasons the domain of money is mostly controlled by men, and women are still told to not "worry their pretty heads" about it. Even today, the North American financial sector is considered a bastion of men.

The Bottom Line. Although women need power and want power, they both fear it and avoid using it. This is because as a society we not only teach girls to shun power we actively encourage them to give it away. We are told that we must always put others first and must never appear more important or powerful than a man. We reinforce these messages by shaming women who display powerful behaviors, calling them pushy, bossy or bitchy and by treating the most powerful women in harshly critical ways, and holding them to the highest standards. Women who dare to have intelligence, money, status and power – or use it – take a very big risk. We should not be surprised when most women shrink and hide when the word "power" is raised. By teaching women to avoid, fear and refrain from using their power we hold them back.

What To Do. We need to understand why we are ambivalent and fearful of power. We must un-do the teaching of women and tell them about the importance of power. We must stop shaming them for wanting or wielding power. We must celebrate powerful women and also stand behind them when they take risks. We must end the brutal portrayals and treatment of powerful women. We must no longer hide from conversations about women and power. We must shift our mind-sets so that we believe that women both deserve and want more power. It's absurd to believe that by giving women power, men will have less power. We must decide that women need more power and we must create ways to hand it to them more easily.

Chapter 19

Never Say Women Have Come Far Enough

> "To be a powerful woman in white Western culture is to be labeled unnatural and unwomanly. To feel deeply, empathizing with the joy and pain of others is to be over-emotional. To be intuitive is to be unscientific – a denial of rationality. To be pretty is to be a bimbo. To be muscular is to be a dyke. To be round and yielding is to be fat. How can we be sensual, in our bodies, if we perpetually deny their beauty? How can we enjoy the feminine roundness of our forms if our image of the good body is that of a preadolescent boy, all angles instead of curves?" ~ Joan Borysenko

Almost every time I mention that I am writing a book on women and power, I am told, "But women have come so far!" Almost everyone wants to convince me that women have come far enough. But, as I say, far enough for whom? It's definitely not far enough for me or for my daughters.

We celebrate a handful of women leaders, not even noticing that we can count these women on one hand. Our business magazines are filled with the faces of hundreds of men who are winning awards and kudos for changing the world. Indeed headshots of men typically out-number women about ten to one.

When women do grace the front business pages, they are rarely celebrated. Recall the cruel media coverage of Martha Stewart, Hillary Clinton and Margaret Thatcher. Indeed, when Anita Roddick, one of the world's most famous entrepreneurs and the CEO and creator of The Body Shop, died a few years ago, her obituary did not appear on a front page.

We forget that the few women who do make it to the top are not only rare but have to make huge sacrifices and break through many barriers. They suffer huge costs to their personal lives and often abandon all non-work-related interests. Yet we still want to think any woman can do it.

So although the facts say otherwise, we have a very hard time admitting things are that bad. We prefer to think that things are moving forward and that everything will work out. Unfortunately, this very thinking is one of the biggest barriers facing women. If we are not willing to admit that women are floundering, it will be almost impossible to bring about change.

So why do we keep lying to ourselves? Although there are many reasons why we are stuck in this state of blissful ignorance, there are three basic and very human reasons why we do not want to admit to the truth about women and prefer to say we are doing fine.

First, it makes us feel bad to admit the truth. Second, we fear confrontation or rocking the boat. And third, we don't really want women to hold power.

Every day I feel bad. I feel horrible about the circumstances of women in the world today. I feel sick when I read about the quiet despair of mothers who are broke and have no power or control over their lives. I turn off the radio when the topic relates to female mutilation or rape. So I understand completely when women turn away from me. It feels uncomfortable hearing about all this negative stuff. I understand completely when women prefer to turn a blind eye to women's problems, particularly when they seem insurmountable. It's all too much. This pain actually causes women to disassociate or deny it's even a problem.

So instead of talking about women's struggles, we instead focus on positive things. This way we feel better, are happier and, as luck would have it, don't complain and make things worse for others.

Indeed, our desire to stay happy drives a billion-dollar media magazine industry that displays only beauty and fluff. Every day, the media machine pumps out tons of crap that makes you feel good and keeps your attention off important issues. Magazines are full of stories of individual successful women who have inherited their fathers' businesses or have finally obtained a high-paying career. But we never hear about the majority of women who are eking out a living and stuck in kitchens. It feels good to believe that women have enough power, and stories about struggling women are frankly depressing.

We give women what they ask for and entice them with beauty, fashion, food and spa retreats. We encourage them to waste their time on short-term gains while staying ignorant of the very things that could result in long-term advances. This phenomenon was labeled the new "opium of the masses" by media critics Noam Chomsky and Edward Herman, who suggested in their book, *Manufacturing Consent,* that governments and big business love the idea of keeping the masses focused on things (like sports events) so that their attention is not on critiquing them.

And to make ourselves feel even better, we compare ourselves to our mothers and grandmothers and think we are so lucky. By comparison, our problems appear to be minor inconveniences. We silence ourselves by saying things like "surely you have nothing to complain about." This positive thinking not only pacifies us but actually makes us feel like we are lucky.

In addition to not wanting to feel bad, we tend to refrain from speaking out because we dislike conflict. We don't like fighting. Even though every woman wants more equality for women, most don't want to do anything that might be too messy — like a revolt. We think that if we say anything about women's rights we will be seen as confrontational.

But, as we all know, this happy and contented state is short-lived. One day we wake up and see that we are not all that powerful and that our choices are not entirely within our hands. As mothers, we feel bad for not having done something when we see our daughters in abusive relationships.

And the third reason we stay silent is because we may not as a society be ready for women to have power. We may not want them to advance at all. We may truly be ambivalent to women in power. When too many women are leaders it just feels weird. We can't explain why, but we don't really think they belong in high-level positions. We don't know what it is, but we don't really think they should be leading countries and corporations. We can't articulate it, but often wonder what will happen if women stop looking after the rest of us.

And this ambivalence is the very deepest reason we hold women back. We have fallen for the idea that if we allow women power, our world as we know it might just fall apart. This is the so-called "rhino under the table" – the conversation absolutely no one wants to have.

These subconscious thoughts about women and power form a type of collective ambivalence and it is based on thousands of years of human conditioning and programming. We have these thoughts in our heads without even realizing it, and it is holding women back.

Some of these thoughts have surfaced in research by Sidra Stone, author of *The Shadow King*. Stone describes some of the traditional thoughts many men and women still have about women and power. Here are a few of her examples

- A real woman doesn't want power.
- If she takes her power, she's acting like a man and she's not really a woman.
- Men are not proud of a woman who is successful in business.

- She's a woman. She shouldn't even try. She'll just fall on her face.

- She must have slept with someone to get where she did.

- Women's businesses never work out. They're okay for little boutiques, but that's all.

- It's just a fluke [about a woman's major success in a traditionally male] job.

- Her father must have gotten her the job.

Related to this is our simple fear of change. There is no doubt that if women did move into more powerful positions, things would change. Having women in power will shift the way we look at things and do things. Women might call things into question or make us more accountable. This can be terrifying for those who prefer to maintain the status quo.

This may be the main reason we have kept women out of power for all of our history. They have slowly scratched away, getting the vote and a few good jobs. All this change has been a long, hard push. And although all these changes have been better for women and better for society, we continue to hold women back.

The Bottom Line. We like to believe that women are powerful, even though the evidence says otherwise. Although women are barely advancing and are in many ways slipping back, women often stay silent – for three reasons. We prefer to stay positive and believe that things aren't that bad; we fear conflict or making a ruckus and we are ambivalent to powerful women. Our desire to ignore the problem is encouraged by a billion-dollar media industry that replaces our angst with materialism – selling beauty and fashion while hiding the harsh reality of the majority of women. This opium, plus our fear of rocking the boat, keeps women passive and prevents us from participating in long-term improvements to women's lives. It also feeds our deeply held thoughts that perhaps women don't want or deserve power. Maybe women weren't meant to be powerful.

What To Do. We have to face the fact that women are not equal or powerful and have not come far enough. We must stop trying to convince women that they have enough power or that they don't need it. We must educate women and men on the ways that pacify women and must stop the harmful media messages immediately. Most importantly we must question our deep subconscious thoughts that make us think that women don't want or deserve power. We must all say out loud: "Yes, women need more power and I will work to help them get that."

Chapter 20

Value Feminine Strengths

> "[W]omen learn communication behaviors that reflect their role in society. They are taught to be soft-spoken and demure around the opposite sex. However, the business world is no place to be ladylike – whatever that means. The soft, breathy Marilyn Monroe voice might have its place, but not in the boardroom. It makes you appear timid, shy, and unsure of yourself, which impacts your credibility and professionalism." ~ Susan Solovic

Last year I gave a talk to a group of university women titled "Feminine Intelligence: The Seven Hidden Strengths of Women." In preparation I went to my husband and asked him the things about me that bothered him most. When he had come up with his list, I mapped these things onto my research on women and power. I was completely surprised to see that the very things I was criticized for were actually what I came to call my feminine strengths. Here are a few examples.

- Women talk too much versus we are excellent communicators and relationship builders.

- Women are unfocused versus we consider things from several different perspectives.

- Women depend too much on others' advice versus we are collaborative and considerate.

- Women want to be liked versus we are empathetic, kind and good listeners.

When I shared this list with other women, huge lights began to go on. The very things that women excelled in were the things that often attracted the most criticism.

The following comment by Susan Solovic provides an example of how we label women as behaving inappropriately: "Women like to talk about relationships and feelings. Our conversations are filled with personal details, descriptive adjectives, and superfluous words. For the most part, however, that type of intimacy is not appropriate in business communications."

Women are regularly accused of being too emotional, too talkative, too nice, etc. As well, many of the jobs requiring these strengths are criticized and devalued. Jobs like nursing, care giving, teaching and managing people. These jobs involve so-called "soft skills" that can comfortably be overlaid on women's natural propensities. In workplaces, however, these assets are often seen as weaknesses and problematic.

By shifting our thinking we would realize that both feminine and masculine attributes and preferences are ideal. For example, you would likely want to hire a person with the following characteristics:

- Can form and maintain healthy relationships.
- Can demonstrate empathy, compassion and kindness.
- Is able to listen, paraphrase and acknowledge others.
- Is sensitive to displays of emotion, even if not verbal.
- Can resolve conflicts for self and others through speaking and mediating.
- Enjoys working in a group, collaborating and sharing with others.

As author Anita Roberts says:

In a society that is run by men and shines a bright light on the achievements of men, it is important to look at what females do better than males. This is not a way of putting men down but a way of focusing on the gifts that girls and women have and perhaps questioning why males in our society hold the majority of the power. It is important for females to tell the truth about their experience without feeling they are putting men down.

There is little doubt that in our society masculine traits are considered more valuable. These two columns compare some of the more generic, so-called feminine and masculine values.

Feminine Values	Masculine Values
Respect	Control
Equality	Hierarchy
Empowering	Competing
Collaboration	Dominance
Process	End results
Nurturing	Exploitation
Tender	Tough
Dialogue	Advocacy
Open	Focused
Creativity	Persistence
Adaptability	Manipulation
Purpose	Ambition
Interconnectivity	Divisions
Chaos	Predictability
Contribution	Industry
Morality	Ethics and codes of conduct
Power within	Power over
Restoration	Punishment
Intuition	Scientific rigor
Spirituality	Religion
Community	Individualism

It can be quite difficult for men or women to start seeing feminine values as a positive thing when we have been raised in a culture that not only often denies them but distorts them and devalues them, so much so that it might feel shameful or embarrassing for us to even talk about them. We laugh at those who say they are intuitive; we shame those who place too much emphasis on relationships.

It should come as no surprise then that our workplaces are so sterile and inhuman with individuals being asked to behave like emotionless robots who are not to be concerned about others. The irony is that the hottest, best-selling business books are on emotional and social intelligence. After centuries of being told that emotions do not matter and are actually harmful, we now realize their value and thus have to relearn how to feel!

This continual rejection of women and their essential values and skills is what leads to women feeling invisible or unheard – often called "invisible women syndrome." Solovic describes it as follows:

> It is the saga of the invisible woman. Women are invisible because of personal bias – an attitude that women aren't serious players in the business world. Some Neanderthal men refuse to accept women as coworkers, bosses, or decision makers. Therefore, anything we have to say gets filtered through a screen on antiquated perceptions, and by the time it is actually received, it has little significance.

One common experience that reflects this phenomenon is called the "stolen idea." Here is what happens to many women. During a meeting a woman will make a suggestion or offer a new idea. Her idea is ignored or brushed aside. A few minutes later a man in the group will offer the identical suggestion. It will be embraced by the group. Often the man does not realize that the woman has already suggested it. The woman can't figure out why no one heard her when she said it and is peeved that it was stolen without any acknowledgment.

Related to this is the so-called "imposter syndrome" or "fraud complex" that so many professional women suffer from. It results directly from this conditioning, telling us that women do not belong therefore they must be frauds to have gotten so far. Many women are convinced that they will be discovered and tossed out on their heads, so they keep working furiously, never questioning the fact that they are killing themselves.

In her book *The Dance of the Dissident Daughter*, Sue Monk Kidd describes it as follows: "I've spent my whole life trying hard not to drop the ball, trying to make it up to my father for being nothing but a girl, hoping I could finally get him to prize me like he did my brother. The crazy thing is, I have a 19-page resume, but still there is this little voice inside me telling me I'm going to mess up."

> **The Bottom Line.** Women are continually told that their feminine tendencies, skills and values are inappropriate. Women are told that they are too emotional, too concerned about others, too sensitive, too collaborative. When these strengths are criticized women often feel unheard and invisible. And when women do succeed, many feel like imposters. As a result women begin to question themselves at a fundamental level, resulting in reduced confidence and lower self-esteem. Yet, as research shows, these so-called feminine strengths are the very things that have been missing from corporations. By condemning them we not only crush women but make our workplaces sterile and lopsided.

What To Do. We need to be aware of the ways we criticize the very strengths of women. We need to re-claim these strengths and re-cast them so that they can be embraced rather than rejected. This includes emotional intelligence, social intelligence, intuition, empathy, caring, collaboration, connecting, to name a few. I would encourage everyone to read one of my favorite books by Dayle Smith, *Women at Work*. She simplifies the research that supports these ideas and reinforces the idea that women's behaviors, which often get judged negatively, are actually very powerful and useful.

Conclusion

> "Men aren't going to shift simply because we want them to; after all, they created the traditional structures to suit themselves. For most men, an increase in women's status is seen to hold no benefit... we need to actively address the systems men have created." ~ Stephanie Vermeulen

My ultimate goal in writing this book was to help bring about equality – quickly. I wanted to make sure that *anyone* could quickly understand what was happening to women and immediately take action. I really wanted to make academic knowledge accessible to all women so they could improve their lives, right now.

This book shows the many ways in which our corporate institutions, policies and biases hold women back. We expect women to act like mini-men and burden them with absurd expectations. We squeeze them into outdated stereotypes and hold them in double binds. Then we tell them that their problems are of their own making and they either need to get more courage, work harder or leave. These barriers not only harm women but our whole society.

Here is a quick summary of what I have said in this book:

- Women have not achieved equality although they have been fighting for equal opportunities and fair treatment for hundreds of years;

- Women are valuable assets to corporations, to business, to industry and to society;

- Our outdated institutions, policies and biases are holding women back;

- Asking women to engage in individual self-help is not enough to bring about equality; and

- Both men and women need to recognize and remove the barriers that hold women back.

To bring about lasting change we first need to stop asking women to change. We must invite men, women, corporations and governments to work together to bring about more equitable workplaces. We must stop calling the barriers that women face a "women's issue" and instead call it a "corporate issue."

I recommend that every company, organization or firm do the following.

Step 1. Commit to making change. Each organization must admit that women face particular barriers and that the corporate model is part of the problem. Each president, CEO and Board must commit to advancing women and put this in writing. This means not just tinkering but rather creating an inclusive culture that welcomes women and particularly mothers. This statement should be made public and distributed to all employees, clients and stakeholders. As you do this, it would make sense to educate employees and others about the many barriers (e.g., provide copies of this book). At the minimum it is useful to share something like the words of Professor Joan C. Williams and Rachel Dempsey:

> We now have some concrete answers about why women don't reach the highest levels in proportionate numbers. Men get promoted based on fewer accomplishments than women would need to reach the same level. Women are more likely than men to be penalized if they make a mistake. And when women have children, they need to start proving themselves all over again — and to cope with disapproval from colleagues who believe, explicitly or unconsciously, that a mother who is

still highly committed to her career is failing as a mother. If women need to accomplish twice as much to get half as far and accomplishments are distributed evenly among men and women, it stands to reason that women don't reach the top. But that's not all. Even highly accomplished women face office politics that are far trickier than office politics faced by men.

Step 2. Create specific goals. Each organization must create goals and strategies to ensure the commitment is fulfilled. One easy way to do this is by using the 20 strategies in the book which are summarized at the back. A first step would be to simply measure the extent to which the organization is currently achieving each one. For example, you may be faring well in dealing with harassment but not so much in promoting women. From this assessment it is easy to write more specific desired outcomes, actions and goals that can then be measured.

Step 3. Implement a sustainable process. The system that is designed to implement the goals is just as important as the goals themselves. The process must look like a circular system of continual improvement that does not depend on one person or department. There must be continual collection of information about the advancement of women, input from all employees and a way to monitor the success of the goals and report back. The process must be self-sustainable.

If you really want to empower women the very first step is easy. Simply share what you have learned in this book. Give this book to another woman or man or buy a copy for a friend or workmate.

Share the 20 strategies at the end of this book (*Lean Out – A Manifesto for Work Equality*). Copy the list and distribute it to your boss and colleagues. Share it with your networks (contact the author for an electronic version) and simply have conversations. That's how every change begins with you.

And if you want lasting change give this book to your sons and daughters so that they have the information needed to become a new generation of equality-minded citizens.

Lean Out:
A Manifesto for Work Equality

20 Strategies

1. Admit there is a glass ceiling
2. Stop telling women to lean in
3. Don't fall for the pipeline theory
4. Ask women why they really leave
5. Notice the absurd expectations we place on women
6. Question the tightrope of double binds
7. Don't expect women to be mini-men
8. Question why women need more courage
9. Reject outdated stereotypes
10. Stop asking women to speak louder
11. Pay and promote women fairly
12. Make flexible, part-time and shared work the norm
13. Don't blame women for self-sabotage
14. Deal with discrimination and sexism
15. Stop sexual harassment
16. Provide access to mentors, networks and women
17. Provide support for life and family
18. Encourage women to seek power
19. Never say women have come far enough
20. Value feminine strengths

Copyright @Maureen F. Fitzgerald; *Lean Out: How to Dismantle the Corporate Barriers that Hold Women back.* For electronic copies please contact the author at www.MaureenFitzgerald.com.

Appendix A

The Business Case for Advancing Women

The following is a sample of the research that shows that by having more women at higher levels of organizations, companies are better able to leverage talent, improve financial performance and improve organizational health.

- The *Harvard Business Review:* Dedicated its September 2013 issue to describing not only the barriers that women face at work but also the benefits to companies that had policies to advance women. https://hbr.org/2013/09/women-rising-the-unseen-barriers.

- *McKinsey & Company*: Has been conducting research on the topic of diversity in the workplace annually for many years. Their first report, "Women Matter" (2007), identified a positive relationship between corporate performance and elevated presence of women in the workplace in several Western European countries. For several years since, various annual "Women Matters" studies have shown that those companies with a "critical mass" of female executives perform better that those with no women in top management. One recent study surveyed 1400 managers from a wide range of companies worldwide and discovered that corporate culture is critical to women's advancement. Indeed it is twice as important as individual mind-sets in determining whether women succeed. McKinsey & Company recommended the following four things companies must do to reach greater gender diversity:

    - Educate men about the specific difficulties women face in reaching the top.

- Embrace diversity in leadership and communication styles.

- Challenge women's perception that female leadership styles do not fit in the prevailing styles.

- Question the "anytime anywhere" performance model that is seen by both genders to penalize women and put men at an advantage.

www.mckinsey.com/~/media/McKinsey/dotcom/homepage/2012_March_Women_Matter/PDF/WomenMatter%202013%20Report.ashx

- *The Conference Board of Canada*: Conducted research and found that gender diversity in senior management is good for organizations. The report "Women in Leadership: Perceptions and Priorities for Change" (2014) noted that women's presence at senior levels improves decision-making, operational and financial results, and other factors. http://www.conferenceboard.ca/e-library/abstract.aspx?did=5150

- *The Conference Board of Canada:* Found that the representation of women on corporate boards improves financial performance, enables recruitment of top talent and better understanding of clients' needs, heightens innovation, and improves board effectiveness. http://www.conferenceboard.ca/ topics/gcsr/wob.aspx

- *Catalyst:* Tracked the performance of Fortune 500 companies between 2004 and 2008 and found that companies with the most female directors outperformed those with the fewest. They yielded 26% higher return on invested capital and 16% higher return on sales. http://www.catalyst.org/knowledge/bottom-line-corporate-performance-and-womens-representation-boards

- *Catalyst*: Found that gender-diverse boards are good for business and society. Companies with both women and men in the boardroom are better equipped to oversee corporate actions and ensure corporate citizenship standards are not only met, but exceeded, building stronger, more sustainable companies. http://www.catalyst.org/knowledge/companies-behaving-responsibly-gender-diversity-boards

- *Gallop:* Looked at characteristics of great managers based on over four decades of extensive talent research and studied 2.5 million manager-led teams in 195 countries and about 27 million employees. "The State of the American Manager Report" (2012) shows that female managers outperform male managers on employee engagement scores. The report examines the crucial link among talent, engagement and vital business outcomes, including profitability and productivity. http://www.gallup.com/services/182216/state-american-manager-report.aspx#

Appendix B

The Women's Leadership Gap. Women's Leadership by the Numbers

By Judith Warner, Center for American Progress, 4 August 2015

This fact sheet is an updated version of "The Women's Leadership Gap," published on March 7, 2014. In the intervening period, Catalyst – the source of most of the data on women's representation on boards and in executive positions in the United States – began to chart women's representation in Standard&Poor's 500 companies rather than Fortune 500 companies. Readers should be aware of this shift when comparing the statistics here to those reported last year.

Women make up a majority of the U.S. population

Women are 50.8 percent of the U.S. population.

- They earn almost 60 percent of undergraduate degrees and 60 percent of all master's degrees.

- They earn 47 percent of all law degrees and 48 percent of all medical degrees.

- They earn more than 38 percent of master's degrees in business and management, including 36 percent of MBAs, and 47 percent of specialized master's degrees.

- They account for 47 percent of the U.S. labor force and 49 percent of the college-educated workforce.

And yet...

Although they hold almost 52 percent of all professional-level jobs, American women lag substantially behind men when it comes to their representation in leadership positions:

- While they are 45 percent of the overall S&P 500 labor force and 37 percent of first or mid-level officials and managers in those companies, they are only 25 percent of executive- and senior-level officials and managers, hold only 19 percent of board seats, and are only 4.6 percent of CEOs.

- At S&P 500 companies in the financial services industry, they make up 54 percent of the labor force but are only 19 percent of board directors and 2 percent of CEOs.

- In the legal field, they are 45 percent of associates but only 20 percent of partners and 17 percent of equity partners.

- In medicine, they comprise 35.5 percent of all physicians and surgeons but only 16 percent of permanent medical school deans.

- In academia, they are only 30 percent of full professors and 26 percent of college presidents.

- They are only 6 percent of partners in venture capital firms – down from 10 percent in 1999.

- In 2014, their representation in technology jobs at nine major Silicon Valley companies ranged from a low of 10 percent at Twitter to a high of 27 percent at Intuit. As recently as spring 2014, nearly 47 percent of the 150 highest-earning public companies in Silicon Valley had no female executive officers at all.

Furthermore…

Women's on-screen image is still created, overwhelmingly, by men:

- Women accounted for just 17 percent of all the directors, executive producers, producers, writers, cinematographers, and editors who worked on the top-grossing 250 domestic films of 2014.

- Women were just 27 percent of all off-screen talent on broadcast television programs during the 2013-14 primetime season.

- However, when there are more women behind the camera or at the editor's desk, the representation of women onscreen is better: Films written or directed by women consistently feature a higher percentage of female characters with speaking roles.

A stalled revolution

The last decades of the 20th century brought considerable progress in women's professional advancement in the United States. The gender wage gap narrowed, sex segregation in most professions greatly declined, and the percentage of women climbing the management ranks steadily rose. Although the rapid rate of change of the 1970s and 1980s began to slow in the 1990s and 2000s, as the narrowing of the gender wage gap stalled and the percentage of women in management jobs stagnated, a notable increase in women's representation in very top positions did continue:

- In 1980, there were no women in the top executive ranks of the Fortune 100; by 2001, 11 percent of those corporate leaders were women.

- Women's share of board seats in S&P 1500 companies increased 7.2 percentage points, or 94 percent, from 1997 to

2009, and their share of top executive positions increased 2.8 percentage points, or 86 percent. The share of companies with female CEOs increased more than sixfold.

In recent years, however, the percentage of women in top management positions and on corporate boards has stalled:

- As recently as 2011, their presence in top management positions in S&P 1500 companies was less than 9 percent.

- Although there has been a slow but steady increase, progress for women is uneven; while 19 percent of S&P 500 board directors are women, only 15 percent of directors of S&P mid-cap companies are women, compared to 12.6 percent of directors of S&P small-cap companies.

- Overall, just 15.8 percent of directors of S&P 1500 companies are women.

- Companies with female CEOs tend to have more female directors; however, as of October, 2014, there were only 67 female CEOs in the S&P 1500.

Women of color face an even wider gap

The representation of women of color in corporate leadership roles is worse still. Women of color were 38 percent of the nation's female population and 19 percent of the entire U.S. population in 2014. In 2013, they made up 36 percent of the female labor force and 17 percent of the total labor force and are currently 16.5 percent of workers in S&P 500 companies.

And yet...

- Women of color are only 3.9 percent of executive- or senior-level officials and managers in those companies.

- Women of color hold only 3.1 percent of the board seats of Fortune 500 companies – a number that exaggerates their actual presence, as fully one-quarter of the board members who are women of color serve on multiple boards.

- As recently as 2013, more than two-thirds of Fortune 500 companies had no women of color as board directors at all.

How does the United States measure up to other countries?

In private-sector women's leadership, not so badly: the United States ranks number four in women's economic participation and opportunity on the World Economic Forum's 2014 Gender Gap Index of 142 countries.

But in the public sector – and in the percentage of female legislators in particular – the United States lags far behind many countries:

- The United States currently ranks 54th in women's political empowerment on the Gender Gap Index; Iceland, Finland, Norway, and Nicaragua lead the way.

- The world average for the share of women in the lower houses of national parliaments is 22.5 percent – slightly above the 19.4 percent in the U.S. House of Representatives.

- For a country such as the United States with a winner-take-all voting system rather than a system of proportional representation and no quotas, estimates suggest that it will take until near the end of this century to reach 40 percent legislative participation by women.

U.S. women in politics: Much promise, less change

In the 1980s and early 1990s, the percentage of women running for office increased steadily, culminating in the so-called Year of the

Woman in 1992, when the number of women in the U.S. Senate suddenly doubled – from two to four – and the number of women in Congress increased from 28 to 47.

In more recent election cycles, however, the percentage of female candidates has essentially plateaued. In the decade leading up to 2012, the number of women elected to Congress remained basically flat, and the number of women in state legislatures actually decreased.

2012 was considered a watershed election year for women in American politics:

- After a series of historic wins, there were no longer any male-only state legislatures.

- New Hampshire, notably, sent an all-female delegation to Congress and elected a female governor.

- Six additional women of color were elected to the House of Representatives, bringing their total number in Congress to a record of 28.

- Female candidates raised as much money, and were as successful in their election bids, as male candidates running for public office.

In the 2014 midterm elections, the number of women in Congress finally reached triple digits. The 104 women of the 114th Congress include:

- Five new women of color in the House of Representatives, including Rep. Mia Love of Utah, the first black female Republican ever elected to that body

- Sen. Joni Ernst (R), the first women ever elected to either house of the U.S. Congress from Iowa and the first female veteran to serve in the U.S. Senate

- Sen. Shelley Moore Capito (R), the first female senator from West Virginia

In addition, Rhode Island elected its first woman governor, Gina Raimondo (D).

And yet...

- The 2014 gain in new congressional seats held by women was accompanied by the loss of a lot of female power. As the 114th Congress convened, the number of U.S. Senate committees chaired by women fell to two from nine in the 113th Congress.

- Women were a smaller percentage of the vote in the 2014 midterm elections than in 2012 and 2010.

- Women today hold only 24.3 percent of seats in state legislatures.

- They are only 12 percent of governors and only 17 percent of the mayors of the 100 largest American cities.

- Women of color represent only 6.2 percent of the total members of Congress.

- Women of color make up 4.0 percent of governors and 5.2 percent of state legislators.

In sum

Women have outnumbered men on college campuses since 1988. They have earned at least one-third of law degrees since 1980 and accounted for fully one-third of medical school students by 1990. Yet they have not moved up to positions of prominence and power in America at anywhere near the rate that should have followed.

In a broad range of fields, their presence in top leadership positions – as equity law partners, medical school deans, and corporate executive officers – remains stuck at a mere 10 percent to 20 percent. Their "share of voice" – the average proportion of their representation on op-ed pages and corporate boards; as TV pundits, Wikipedia contributors, Hollywood writers, producers, and directors; and as members of Congress – is just 18 percent.

In fact, it has been estimated that, at the current rate of change, it will take until 2085 for women to reach parity with men in key leadership roles in the United States.

Judith Warner is a Senior Fellow at the Center for American Progress.
Source: Tuesday, August 4, 2015, www.americanprogress.org

Selected Bibliography

Babcock, Linda and Sara Laschever. *Women Don't Ask: The High Cost of Avoiding Negotiation and Strategies for Change.* Bantam Dell, 2007.

Bennetts, Leslie. *The Feminine Mistake: Are We Giving Up Too Much?* Hyperion, 2007.

De Beauvoir, Simone. *The Second Sex.* Knopf, 1953.

Canadian Board Diversity Council. *Annual Report Card.* 2012.

Catalyst. "Advancing Women Leaders: The Connection Between Women Board Directors and Women Corporate Officers." Catalyst, 2008.

Catalyst. "Catalyst Census: Financial Post Women on Board Directors." Catalyst, 2012.

Catalyst. "Catalyst Quick Take: Sex Discrimination and Sexual Harassment." May 28, 2015.

Catalyst. "The *2013 Catalyst* Census: *Fortune* 500 Women Executive Officers and Top Earners." Catalyst 2013.

Catalyst. "The Bottom Line: Corporate Performance and Women's Representation on Boards (2004-2008)." Catalyst, 2011.

Dee, Catherine. *A Girls' Guide to Life: Take Charge of Your Personal Life, Your School Time, Your Social Scene, and Much More!* Little Brown, 2005.

Dolan-Del Vecchio, Ken. *Making Love, Playing Power. Men, Women and the Rewards of Intimate Justice.* Soft Skull Press, 2008.

Douglas, Susan J. and Meredith W. Michaels. *The Mommy Myth: The Idealization of Motherhood and How It Has Undermined All Women.* Free Press, 2004.

Eisler, Riane. *The Power of Partnership: Seven Relationships that Will Change Your Life.* New World Library, 2002.

———. *The Chalice and the Blade: Our History, Our Future.* Harper San Francisco, 1988.

———. *The Real Wealth of Nations: Creating a Caring Economics.* Berrett-Koehler, 2007.

Ellison, Sheila (ed.) and Marie Wilson. *If Women Ruled the World: How to Create the World We Want to Live In.* New World Library, 2004.

Elium, Jeanne and Don Elium. *Raising a Daughter: Parents and the Awakening of a Healthy Woman.* Celestial Arts, 2003.

Engberg, Karen. *It's Not the Glass Ceiling: It's the Sticky Floor. And Other Things Our Daughters Should Know about Marriage, Work, and Motherhood.* Prometheus, 1999.

Evans, Gail. *She Wins, You Win: The Most Important Rule Every Business Woman Needs to Know.* Gotham, 2003.

Faludi, Susan. *Backlash: The Undeclared War Against American Women.* Anchor, 1992.

Fitzgerald, Maureen F. *Occupy Women: A Manifesto for Positive Change in a World Run by Men. 20 Powerful Strategies.* Centerpoint Media, 2016.

Frankel, Lois P. *Nice Girls Don't Get the Corner Office: 101 Unconscious Mistakes Women Make that Sabotage their Careers.* Warner Books, 2010.

Friedan, Betty. *The Feminine Mystique.* Norton, 1963.

Greenberg, Selma. *Right from the Start. A Guide to Non-sexist Child Rearing.* Houghton Mifflin, 1979.

Hewlett, Sylvia A. "Off Ramps and On Ramps: Keeping Talented Women on the Road to Success," *Harvard Business Review Press*, 2007.

——— and Cornel West. *The War Against Parents: What We Can Do for America's Beleaguered Moms and Dads.* Houghton Mifflin, 1998.

Hochschild, Arlie R. and Anne Machung. *The Second Shift.* Penguin, 2003.

Kellerman, Barbara and Deborah Rhode. *Women and Leadership: The State of Play and Strategies for Change.* Jossey-Bass, 2007.

Kidd, Sue Monk. *Dance of the Dissident Daughter: A Women's Journey from Christian Tradition to the Sacred Feminine.* Harper, 1996.

Kunin, Madeline. *The New Feminist Agenda: Defining the Next Revolution for Women, Work, and Family.* Chelsea Green Publishing, 2012.

Maier, Corinne. *No Kids. 40 Good Reasons Not to Have Children.* McLelland & Stewart, 2009.

McKinsey & Company. *Women Matter: Gender Diversity a Corporate Performance Driver.* McKinsey & Company, 2007.

———. *Women Matter, 2013: Gender Diversity in Top Management: Moving Corporate Culture, Moving Boundaries.* McKinsey & Company, 2013.

Meers, Sharon and Joanna Strober. *Getting to 50/50: How Working Parents Can Have it All.* Viva Editions, 2013.

Miles, Rosalind. *Who Cooked the Last Super: The Women's History of the World.* Broadway Books, 2001.

Moen, Phyllis and Patricia Roehling. *Career Mystique: Cracks in the American Dream.* Rowman and Littlefield, 2004.

O'Reilly, Andrea. *Mother Outlaws: Theories and Practices of Empowered Mothering.* Women's Press, 2004.

Perlow, Leslie. *Finding Time: How Corporations, Individuals, and Families Can Benefit from New Work Practices.* Ilr Pr, 2007.

Rhode, Deborah. *The Unfinished Agenda: Women and the Legal Profession.* American Bar Association Commission on the Status of Women, 2001.

Rice, Curt. "The Motherhood Penalty: It's not Children that Slow Mothers Down." December 8, 2011, accessed August 3, 2015 at http://curt-rice.com/2011/12/08/the-motherhood-penalty-its-not-children-that-slow-mothers-down/.

Rich, Adrienne. *Of Woman Born: Motherhood as Experience and Institution.* W.W. Norton, 1986.

Rivers, Caryl and Rosalind C. Barnett. *The New Soft War on Women.* Tarcher, 2013.

Roberts, Anita. *Safe Teen: Powerful Alternatives to Violence.* Polestar Books, 2001.

Roth, Louise Marie. *Selling Woman Short: Gender and Money on Wall Street.* Princeton University Press, 2006

Sandberg, Sheryl. *Lean In: Women, Work and the Will to Lead.* Knopf, 2013.

Schaef, Anne Wilson. *Women's Reality: An Emerging Female System in a White Male Society.* Harper & Row, 1985.

Shipman, Claire and Katty Kay. *Womenomics: Write Your Own Rules for Success.* Harper, 2009.

Silverstein, Brett and Deborah Perlick. *The Cost of Competence – Why Inequality Causes Depression, Eating Disorders and Illness in*

Women. Oxford University Press, 1995.

Slaughter, Anne-Marie. "Why Women Can't Have it All," *Atlantic*, July-August 2012 at http://thealtantic.com/magazine/archive/2012/07/.

Smith, Dayle M. *Women at Work: Leadership for the Next Century.* Prentice Hall, 1999.

Solovic, Susan. *The Girls' Guide to Power and Success.* Amacom, 2001.

Stone, Pamela. *Opting Out? Why Women Really Quit Careers and Head Home.* University of California Press, 2007.

Stone, Sidra. *The Shadow King: The Invisible Force that Holds Women Back*. iUniverse, 1997.

Tannen, Deborah. *You Don't Understand: Women and Men in Conversation.* William Morrow, 2007.

———. *Talking from 9-5: Women and Men at Work*. Quill, 1994

The Conference Board of Canada. *Women on Boards: Not Just the Right Thing...But the "Bright" Thing.* The Conference Board of Canada, 2002.

Valenti, Jessica. *He's a Stud, She's a Slut and 49 Other Double Standards Every Woman Should Know*. Seal Press, 2008.

Vermeulen, Stephanie. *Stitched Up: Who Fashions Women's Lives?* Jacana, 2005.

Warner, Judith. *Perfect Madness: Motherhood in the Age of Anxiety.* Riverhead, 2005.

Williams, Joan C. and Rachel Dempsey. *What Women Want at Work: Four Patterns Working Women Need to Know.* New York University Press, 2014.

Williamson, Marianne. *A Woman's Worth.* Ballantine, 1994.

Wolf, Naomi. *The Beauty Myth: How Images of Beauty are Used Against Women.* Doubleday, 1991.

About the Author

Maureen F. Fitzgerald, PhD, JD, LLM, BComm is a recovering lawyer, author and change agent. She practiced law for over 20 years and is the founder of CenterPoint Media, a multimedia publisher of books that advance thinking.

In her former life, Maureen was a labor lawyer, a policy lawyer and a mediator. She was also a professor of law at two universities and has written twelve books and many articles – both academic and practical. She has a business degree, two law degrees, a masters' degree in law from the London School of Economics and a doctorate degree in philosophy.

Always a leader of both people and ideas, Maureen speaks across North America about social justice, equality and mindfulness. Her motto is: *Sharing the right ideas at the right time can change the world.*

Maureen is the author of the following books:

- **Lean Out**: *How to Dismantle the Corporate Barriers that Hold Women Back.*

- **Motherhood is Madness**: *How to Break the Chains that Prevent Mothers from Being Truly Happy.*

- **Occupy Women**: *A Manifesto for Positive Change in a World Run by Men.*

- **A Woman's Circle:** *Create a Peer Mentoring Group for Advice, Networking, Support and Connection.*

- ***Invite the Bully to Tea:*** *End Harassment, Bullying and Dysfunction Forever with a Simple yet Radical New Approach.*

- ***If Not Now, When?*** *Create a Life and Career of Purpose with a Powerful Vision, a Mission Statement and Measurable Goals.*

- ***Mindfulness Made Easy:*** *50 Simple Practices to Reduce Stress, Create Calm and Live in the Moment – At Home, Work and School.*

- ***Hiring, Managing and Keeping the Best:*** *The Complete Canadian Guide for Employers,* with Monica Beauregard.

- ***So You Think You Need a Lawyer:*** *How to Screen, Hire, Manage or Fire a Lawyer.*

- ***Legal Problem Solving:*** *Reasoning, Research and Writing (7ed).* Lexis/Nexis.

- ***Wake up Sleeping Beauty****: Protect Your Daughter from Sexism, Stereotypes and Sexualization [2016].*

- ***Mean Girls Aren't Mean****: Stand up to Cliques, Bullies, Peer Pressure and Popularity and Empower Girls in a Radical New Way [2016].*

- ***Gritty Is the New Pretty:*** *Raise Confident, Courageous and Resilient Girls in a Man's World [2016].*

You can find her at www.MaureenFitzgerald.com.

Other Books in This Series

How to dismantle the corporate barriers that hold women back **LEAN OUT** Maureen F. Fitzgerald, PhD	**How to break the chains that prevent mothers from being truly happy** **MOTHERHOOD IS MADNESS** Maureen F. Fitzgerald, PhD	**A manifesto for positive change in a world run by men** **OCCUPY WOMEN** Maureen F. Fitzgerald, PhD

Made in the USA
Columbia, SC
07 November 2017